DAY-BY-DAY

MATH

DAY- BY-DAY

MATH

ACTIVITIES FOR GRADES 3–6

SUSAN OHANIAN

Math Solutions Publications
Sausalito, CA

Math Solutions Publications
A division of
Marilyn Burns Education Associates
150 Gate 5 Road, Suite 101
Sausalito CA 94965
www.mathsolutions.com

Library of Congress Cataloging-in-Publication Data
Ohanian, Susan.
    Day-by-day math : activities for grades 3–6 / Susan Ohanian.
      p.   cm.
    ISBN 0-941355-28-4 (alk. paper)
    1. Mathematics—Study and teaching (Elementary)   I. Title.

QA135.5 .O327 2000
372.7—dc21

                                  00-58225

Editor: Toby Gordon
Production: Melissa L. Inglis
Cover and interior design: Joni Doherty Design
Cover and interior illustrations: Twyla Bogaard

Printed in the United States of America on acid-free paper
04 03 02 01 00   ML   1 2 3 4 5

A Message from Marilyn Burns

We at Marilyn Burns Education Associates believe that teaching mathematics well calls for continually reflecting on and improving one's instructional practice. Our Math Solutions Publications include a wide range of choices, from books that describe problem-solving lessons, to *Math By All Means* units that show how to teach specific topics, to resources that help link math with writing and literature, to children's books that help students develop an appreciation for math while learning basic concepts.

Along with our large collection of teacher resource books, we have a more general collection of books, videotapes, and audio-tapes that can help teachers and parents bridge the gap between home and school. All of our materials are available at education stores, from distributors, and through major teacher catalogs.

In addition, Math Solutions Inservice offers five-day courses and one-day workshops throughout the country. We also work in partnership with school districts to help implement and sustain long-term improvement in mathematics instruction in all classrooms.

To find a complete listing of our publications and workshops, please visit our Web site at *www.mathsolutions.com.* Or contact us by calling (800) 868-9092 or sending an e-mail to *info@mathsolutions.com.*

We're eager for your feedback and interested in learning about your particular needs. We look forward to hearing from you.

Math SOLUTIONS® Publications

A DIVISION OF MARILYN BURNS EDUCATION ASSOCIATES

CONTENTS

PREFACE

Day-by-Day Math is an eclectic and quirky collection of event anniversaries, two per day, for every day of the year, from January 1 through December 31. Some entries chronicle familiar historical events, while others reveal little-known facts. Some are serious; some are lighthearted. There's something in the book for everyone.

Susan Ohanian chose each entry for this resource book because it suggests a mathematical problem, investigation, or activity suitable for students in grades 3 through 6. The result is a hefty and diverse collection of ideas for adding an extra bit of oomph to math instruction. Some of the classroom suggestions are ideal for five-, ten-, or fifteen-minute math period "openers." Some can be used for longer class investigations. Many are suitable for individual investigations.

Common math themes run throughout the suggestions in the book. Because of the historical aspect of the entries, there is a steady recurrence of "how long ago did this happen" activities to help students develop strategies for calculating mentally. Also, there are many opportunities for students to collect, organize, and graph data, with suggestions for helping younger children learn about the concept of average while challenging older students to analyze means, medians, and modes. Other activities relate to monetary issues, not only providing students experience with computation, but also giving them a sense of the changes in the value of our currency over time. Still other activities support students' mapping skills. Finally, many of the entries engage students in thinking about areas of measurement—length, weight, and temperature among others.

For teachers interested in integrating math with other areas of the curriculum, relating math to the real world, and enriching children's math learning, Day-by-Day Math is a unique reference. It will delight both teachers and students, all year long.

Marilyn Burns

INTRODUCTION

In *Nature's Numbers* (Basic Books 1995), Ian Stewart observes that "The story of calculus brings out two of the main things that mathematics is for: providing tools that let scientists calculate what nature is doing, and providing new questions for mathematicians to sort out to their own satisfaction." Many people refer to these external and internal aspects of mathematics as applied and pure mathematics. Stewart notes his own dissatisfaction with both the adjectives and the separation the terms imply. This is not an issue only for the ivory tower. We want children to know the algorithms; we also want them to understand how and why they get the answers.

Some readers may be upset by the quantity of problems asking children to grind out answers to arithmetic. Others may carp about introducing sophisticated mathematics that third graders can't possibly understand. Children, of course, need both. By introducing baseball and bus routes, planets and pizza into the math classroom we can expand children's perceptions about what math is. We give children lots of practice in performing the basic functions so they will become proficient. We give children glimpses of the wonders of Fibonacci numbers and tessellations and so much more so that they see the beauties of mathematics as well as its practicalities; we do this so children will be filled with awe and so they will also become thoughtful. One of the highlights of my teaching happened as I was reading aloud to my third graders. When I turned the page and revealed the wonderful display of factorials in Mitsumasa Anno's *Mysterious Multiplying Jar*, the children cheered. Imagine eight-year-olds cheering for factorials.

Ian Stewart insists that "One of the strangest features of the relationship between mathematics and the 'real world,' but also one of the strongest, is that good mathematics, *whatever its source*, eventually turns out to be useful." My teaching career, not just this book, is built on this principle. Good classroom moments, no matter how wacky, will turn out to be useful, but we cannot predict ahead of time what will inspire those good moments or just what uses they will serve. What we do know is that the "Aha!" moments occur when people suddenly see the world from a new angle. By starting the day with diverse mathematical moments, we expand the possibilities for these Ahas! Some of these examples of math in the real world will be useful, others not. Which is which for each child can't be decided ahead of time.

One of the clichés of our time is that math is everywhere, in both trivial and profound ways. To move beyond the clichés, we need to demonstrate to children the diversity of our world's mathematical foundations—in everything from the freezing time of Popsicles, to how the Hubble telescope showed us the importance of precise measurement, to the length of time people had to wait in line to see the *Mona Lisa* when she paid us a visit, to those beautiful Fibonaccis. Children who take a plane trip or watch a TV program or eat an ear of corn can't be expected to understand the complexities of how these systems operate, but we can help them appreciate that it is only because people do understand these phenomena that we are able to enjoy their benefits. When children understand that things they take for granted were invented by people with curiosity and understanding, then these children may well become the inventors we will need tomorrow.

I'd like to quote Ian Stewart one more time. He says, "The really important breakthroughs are always unpredictable." He's talking about the dangers of funding research that is only narrowly focused on the application as a goal and ignoring "curiosity-driven" research. I would say the same thing about children. The really important breakthroughs in learning are always unpredictable. We must be very wary of letting the increasingly managerial culture distract us from the importance of curiosity in the classroom. I hope this book inspires curiosity-driven classroom explorations.

J A N U A R Y

JANUARY 1

1878

Richard Knudsen receives a patent for an inclined-plane railway. Featuring two side-by-side tracks running between two towers, the ride is the forerunner of the roller coaster. Gravity pulls the four-passenger cars down gently sloping hills. Elevators then haul the cars and riders up to the opposite tower, where they are released for the return trip.

Facts and figures on Canadian roller coasters are on the official Web site of Coaster Enthusiasts of Canada: *http:/www.chebucto.ns.ca/~ak621/CEC/CEC.html*.

For photos and information on roller coasters and amusement parks around the world, log on to *http://rollercoaster.com*.

American Coaster Enthusiasts is another fun site: *www.aceonline.org*.

Investigate

America's first roller coaster, the Gravity Pleasure Switchback Railway, at Coney Island, New York, holds ten passengers in one car. Its top speed is six miles per hour. At five cents a ride, the coaster earns $600 a day. How many people ride the Switchback every day?

1901

A new country is born when the six British colonies in Australia, which had been claimed for Great Britain by Captain James Cook in 1770, join together as the Commonwealth of Australia.

Investigate
Mental Math: How many years after Australia's "founding" by Captain Cook was the Commonwealth formed?

How do the sizes of Australia and the United States compare?

JANUARY 2
1752

Betsy Ross, the seamstress believed to have sewn the first United States flag, is born.

Investigate
Draw the pattern of stars on the 13-star flag. If you don't remember, log on to *http://www.icss.com/usflag/the.13.star.flag.html*. Then pick a state, find out how large its entry made the Union, and redesign the flag to show that number of stars. Are some numbers easier for flag design than others?
    Explore flags online at *www.stampsonline.com*; *http://www.ushistory.org/betsy/index.html*; and *http://www.law.ou.edu/fedflag.html*.

1907

President Theodore Roosevelt shakes hands with 8,513 people during a reception at the White House. This number stands in *The Guinness Book of World Records* as the record number of handshakes by a public official.

Investigate
If every student in a group of four students shakes hands with every other student in the group, how many handshakes will that be? In a group of two? Six? If every student in class shakes hands with every other student, how many handshakes will that be? Can you discover a pattern for solving this problem for any number of people?

JANUARY 3
1882

Circus showman P. T. Barnum buys the world-famous elephant Jumbo from the London Zoo, paying $10,000. Billed as the "largest elephant in or out of captivity," Jumbo stands 11 feet tall at the shoulders and weighs 6.5 tons. Barnum's claims regarding the animal's size are considerably more extravagant.

Jumbo seems like an ordinary elephant until he is about seven years old. Then he starts eating an enormous amount of food, enormous even for an elephant. Jumbo's diet for one day includes 200 pounds of hay, two bushels of oats, a barrel of potatoes, several quarts of onions, and 12 to 15 loaves of bread.

Investigate
Jumbo is coming to your house for dinner; plan the menu and make a shopping list.

The 1994 Ringling Brothers and Barnum and Bailey Circus "Blue Show" features the following elephants:

Slam	9,200 pounds
Minnie	9,300 pounds
Calcutta	9,100 pounds
Susan	9,200 pounds
Mysore	8,700 pounds
Karan	8,100 pounds
Karnaudi	8,100 pounds
Rebecca	8,500 pounds
Jewel	8,900 pounds
Nicole	7,800 pounds
Putzi	7,400 pounds
Zina	8,500 pounds
King Tusk	14,762 pounds

Would you describe Jumbo's weight as average, greater than average, or less than average? Explain your reasoning.

1882

P. T. Barnum buys Jumbo.

1959

Alaska, called an "icebox" and a "folly" when the United States purchased it from Russia in 1867, is admitted as the 49th state. By 1995, Alaska has over 600,000 residents, with 31.3 percent of Alaskans under age 18, 4.1 percent over age 65, and a median age of 29.4. The only state in 1995 with a lower median age is Utah, at 26.2, with 36.4 percent of the residents under age 18 and 26.2 percent over age 65. Florida's median age is 36.4, with 22.2 percent of its population under age 18 and 18.3 percent over age 65.

Investigate

Using the above statistics, draw some conclusions about the age of the residents of Florida, Alaska, and Utah.

JANUARY 4
1971

Students in Jill Herrick's third-grade class at Big Creek Elementary School in Middleburg Heights, Ohio, begin collecting bottle caps. Every year, third graders add to the collection; 134,664 hours later, they reach their goal of one million bottle caps.

Investigate

How many weeks, months, or years did it take to reach this goal?

How large a storage place would you need to hold this many bottle caps?

How long does it take our school district to spend $1,000,000? How long does it take the U.S. government to spend $1,000,000?

1984

Adrian Dantley, of the Utah Jazz basketball team, ties Wilt Chamberlain's record, successfully completing 28 of 29 free throws in his team's victory over Houston.

Investigate

In baseball, getting a hit one out of three times at bat makes a player a top hitter. What percentage of shots does a top basketball player make?

Hold a free throw tournament (or a beanbag toss). How many attempts are made before your class makes 28 baskets? What's the percentage of baskets made compared to tosses?

JANUARY 5

1903

The first cable across the Pacific Ocean, between San Francisco and Honolulu, a distance of 2,277 nautical miles (2,620 land miles), becomes available for public use. Nautical miles are based on the length of a minute of arc of a great circle of the earth. They are used by sailors, who base their distance measurements on the Earth's longitude.

Investigate

There are other specialized units of measurement. The *pica*, for example, is 4.217518×10^{-3}, or about one sixth of an inch, and is a unit of length employed in the printing industry. Printers know that 1 pica equals 12 points. Interview adults about specialized units of measurement they may know.

1914

Henry Ford creates a sensation by raising the minimum pay of workers in his automobile plants to five dollars a day.

Investigate

Calculate the weekly salary of someone earning Henry Ford's minimum wage in 1914 and someone earning the minimum wage today. What additional information do you need to decide which salary represents the greater spending power?

JANUARY 6

1903

President Theodore Roosevelt writes to his son Kermit, who is away at school, "Tom Quartz is certainly the cunningest kitten I have ever seen." Cats continue to rise to occasional prominence at the White House throughout the century. In the 1990s, Chelsea Clinton's cat Socks receives more than 50,000 letters a year.

Investigate

When Dr. William Grier of San Diego died, he left $415,000 to his two cats. How much cat food will that buy?

1990

A thief in Providence, Rhode Island, steals four 30-pound bags from an armored car. He is caught before he can run very far. The bags are filled with pennies.

Investigate

How much are four 30-pound bags of pennies worth? What about quarters? Dollar bills?

JANUARY 7

1896

Fanny Farmer publishes her *Boston Cooking School Cook Book*. Since Farmer emphasizes the need for precise amounts, she creates the need for a new product: measuring spoons.

1896
Boston, Massachusetts

Investigate

How many teaspoons are in a tablespoon? In a cup? Conduct experiments to find out.

Choose a popular dish, research how this dish is prepared, and bring a recipe, listing precise amounts, to class. Compare the amounts of ingredients in the different recipes.

1925

Gerald Durrell is born. A writer and naturalist, Durrell loves animals so much that he starts his own zoo. "Zoo" is the abbreviation for zoological park or zoological garden, a facility in which exotic animals are kept for the purpose of conservation, education, and recreation.

In the United States today there are 1,400 registered animal exhibitors, including circuses, game ranches, and menageries. (A menagerie is a collection of wild animals kept on display in cages.) Building the appropriate habitat for animals is very expensive. Currently it costs, on average, between $450 and $550 per square foot to build an exhibit in a large city.

To contact zoos online, check out these Web sites: *www.aza.org*; *http://aazk.ind.net*; *http://www.zoonet.org*.

Investigate

Record the kinds of pets you have on Post-it Notes, using separate notes for each kind of pet. Then, organize the Post-it Notes into a class graph. Discuss what the graph reveals about your pets. Which kind are most common? Least common?

Figure out how many square feet of space your pet would require in an exhibit.

JANUARY 8

1959

George, the tallest giraffe on record, arrives at the Chester Zoo in England. When George is nine years old, his "horns" nearly touch the 20-foot-high roof of the giraffe house. George is extra tall, but at 19 feet (5.8 meters), even the average giraffe is far taller than any other animal. It can be twice as tall as the African elephant and more than three times as tall as a grown man. A fully grown giraffe is so tall that its arteries have special valves to help pump blood all the way up to its head.

Investigate

Make a scale drawing of a giraffe.

Find out the average height of a giraffe at birth and determine the percentage of height growth during its lifetime.

Research the average height of 10 kinds of animals and display this information in a graph.

1963

Leonardo da Vinci's *Mona Lisa*, on loan from the Louvre, goes on exhibit in New York City and then travels to Washington, D.C. Before she leaves for home on March 4, nearly one million people wait in line to see the masterpiece.

Although books provide more information and better reproductions, you can "find" the *Mona Lisa* online at the Louvre Web site: *http://www.louvre.fr/louvrea.htm*. This site is fun to use and has been judged the best art museum in cyberspace.

Investigate

How many people saw the *Mona Lisa* each day during her 1963 visit? About how long did each person wait in line?

People complain a lot about waiting in line. Do some investigating. How long is the aver-

age wait in line in the cafeteria? at a fast-food restaurant? in a supermarket? at a bank? at the mall?

JANUARY 9

1793

At 10:06 A.M., Jean Pierre Blanchard and his dog ascend 5,800 feet over Philadelphia in the first hot air balloon flight in the United States. They land in New Jersey at 10:58 A.M. George Washington is among the interested spectators.

Investigate

Mental Math: How long ago did Blanchard make his flight?

Compare Blanchard's altitude with that reached by jet passenger planes today.

1898

The *Daily Press* in Newport News, Virginia, reports that a quart of milk costs six cents. Milk at six cents a quart sounds like quite a bargain. But in 1898 a woman sewing at home for the clothing industry makes 30 cents a day, the average wage of shop girls in Boston is between $5.00 and $6.00 a week, and a mule driver earns $2.75 a day.

Investigate

What is the ratio of the six-cent quart of milk to the average income at the time?

What is the ratio of the price of a quart of milk today to the current minimum wage? How do these two ratios compare?

JANUARY 10

1951

The C102 jetliner makes history, flying from Toronto to Chicago to New York and back. It flies at twice the speed—520 miles—and twice the altitude—36,000 feet—of propeller-driven airplanes. At this altitude, planes are able to fly above unsettled weather.

Investigate

Find out how long it takes to make a typical commercial flight from New York to San Francisco. What is the hourly speed? Is the flight time from San Francisco to New York the same?

1975

During what is dubbed "The Storm of the Century," the wind chill is between –50° and –80° Fahrenheit in Duluth, Minnesota. Weather information online is available at: *http://www.whnt19.com/kidwx* and *http://www.usatoday.com/weather/wfront.htm*.

Investigate

Keep a weather graph charting the temperature for a month. Then find the average temperature for the month. Check an almanac to find out whether this is above or below average.

JANUARY 11

1922

After ten hours of flying lessons, Amelia Mary Earhart, named for her two grandmothers, makes her first solo flight.

Investigate

How many hours do you think it takes to learn to drive a car?

Can you remember how long it took you to learn to ride a bike? How about learning other skills?

Do you think ten hours is enough time to learn to fly a plane? Write a major airline and ask how long their pilots train.

1964

United States Surgeon General Luther Terry issues a statement declaring that smoking is hazardous to one's health, but people continue to smoke. In the 1990s, Americans smoke 951,293 cigarettes every minute.

Investigate

In ten years, how many cigarettes does a pack-a-day smoker smoke? (There are twenty cigarettes in a pack.) Using the cost of cigarettes today, about how much money is spent on cigarettes? Assuming it takes seven minutes to smoke a cigarette, how much of one's life is spent puffing away?

JANUARY 12

1628

Charles Perrault, a Frenchman who goes on to write some of our most beloved fairy tales—including *Cinderella*, *Little Red Riding Hood*, *Puss in Boots*, *Sleeping Beauty*, and *Snow White*—is born. In 1697, he published *Tales of Mother Goose*, a collection of eleven fairy tales.

Investigate

Mental Math: How old was Charles Perrault when *Tales of Mother Goose* was published?

Take a poll to find out your classmates' three favorite fairy tales. Do boys like different fairy tales than girls do?

Figure out how to show both favorite tales and gender preferences in a graph.

1772

Captain James Cook becomes the first person to cross the Antarctic Circle. With his crew of 118, Cook is on a three-year, eighteen-day journey around the world. Cook is paid six shillings (about 14 cents) a day.

Cook crosses the Antarctic Circle (where the latitude is approximately $66\frac{1}{2}$ degrees south of the equator) four times and reaches a latitude of a little more than 71 degrees south of the equator, but he does not find land. He believes "that no man will ever venture farther than I have done, and that the lands which may lie to the south will never be explored." Cook's prediction may have been wrong, but his accomplishment, in a small wooden boat powered by sails, is incredible.

Investigate

About how much did Cook earn on the journey? Discuss whether you think Cook undertook the trip for the money or for some other reason.

JANUARY 13

1808

Salmon Portland Chase, future senator and secretary of the treasury, is born. Chase is such a determined abolitionist that he is known as the "attorney general for runaway Negroes." He is credited with founding the Republican Party, and his picture is on the 10,000-dollar bill.

Investigate

It takes ten 10,000-dollar bills to make $100,000. Figure out how many of each of the following bills are needed to make $100,000: 1,000-dollar bills, 100-dollar bills, 20-dollar bills, 10-dollar bills, 5-dollar bills, 1-dollar bills.

1997

Steve Fossett takes off from Busch Stadium in St. Louis, Missouri, in a balloon called Solo Spirit, hoping to become the first balloonist to fly around the world without landing: 146 hours and 54 minutes later he lands in Piparpur, India. Fossett doesn't succeed in circling the globe, but he does fly farther than any other balloonist, 9,617 miles.

Investigate

How many days was Fossett in the air? How many miles did he travel each day?

Since his first try, Fossett has made several other attempts. Research the results.

JANUARY 14

1984

Tim Collum, of Boyd, Texas, is crowned United States Video Game King in Ottumwa, Iowa. According to the *Sports Illustrated for Kids Omnibus*, 49 percent of girls in the United States spend less than one hour a day playing video games. Almost 37 percent of boys spend two hours or more a day playing video games.

Investigate

How much time do you spend playing video games? Do the boys in your class like video games better than the girls do? Does age make a difference? Take a poll and graph the results.

1988

In San Francisco, Gary Sussman carves a statue celebrating the Forty-Niners (the gold miners of 1849, not the football team!) out of a 6,000-pound block of Ivory soap.

Investigate

Have each student bring to class a new bar of Ivory soap still in its wrapper. Figure out how many individual bars of soap would be needed to make a 6,000-pound block. What could the dimensions of this block of soap be?

JANUARY 15

1861

Elisha Graves Otis receives a patent for his steam elevator with safety features. Today, the World Trade Center in New York City has 99 elevators serving the 50,000 people who work in the building and the 70,000 tourists who visit it daily. The fastest passenger elevators in the world are in the 70-story, 971-feet-tall Yokohama Landmark Tower, in Japan. They travel at a speed equivalent to 28 miles per hour.

Investigate

Mental Math: How long have elevators been around?

How long does it take to travel to the top of the Yokohama Landmark Tower?

1943

The Pentagon, built to house the U.S. Defense Department offices in Arlington, Virginia, is completed. It sits on the largest ground area covered by any office building. Each of the outermost sides is 921 feet long, and the perimeter of the building is about 4,610 feet. Its five stories enclose a floor area of 149.2 acres. The corridors total 17.5 miles in length, and there are 7,754 windows to be cleaned.

Investigate

Come up with similar statistics for your school.

JANUARY 16

1866

Everett Barney patents the first all-metal roller skate; it is fastened to a shoe.

Investigate

Mental Math: How many years have people been roller-skating?

1994

In Christchurch, New Zealand, 16,837 teddy bears and their owners get together for a picnic.

Investigate

Take a poll: How many stuffed animals live in your classmates' homes? What's the average number of stuffed animals per home? What is the most popular stuffed animal?

JANUARY 17

1956

Heartbreak Hotel, Elvis Presley's first hit, is released. Elvis was born on January 8, 1935. Elvis fans can visit the Graceland site: *http://www.elvis-presley.com*.

Investigate

How old was Elvis Presley when *Heartbreak Hotel* was released? How old would he be today?

1988

A saguaro cactus is found in the Maricopa Mountains near Gila Bend, Arizona. Its candelabra-like branches rise 57 feet, $11\frac{3}{4}$ inches. Armless cactuses can measure as high as 78 feet.

Information, including pictures, is available online: *http://www.desertusa.com/july96/du_saguaro.html*.

Investigate

Measure the height of houseplants in your home or in school. How tall is the tallest?

Grow cactuses as a class project. Keep monthly measurements. What is the rate of growth per year?

JANUARY 18

1733

Ursa Major, or the Great Bear, a nine-month-old cub that had been caught in the Davis Strait on the western coast of Greenland, goes on exhibition at Clark's Wharf in Boston. A year later, Ursa is shipped to London in order to be exhibited there.

Investigate

Look at a map and estimate how many miles Ursa traveled to get from Greenland to Boston to London.

1899

Arctic explorer Robert Peary, suffering from severe frostbite, has parts of seven toes removed. Thirteen years later Antarctic explorer Captain Robert F. Scott writes in his journal at the South Pole, "Great God! This is an awful place."

Investigate

Find out the average temperatures at both the North and South Poles. Why are these places so cold?

JANUARY 19

1915

Ernest Shackleton's ship, *Endurance*, becomes trapped in ice at a latitude of 74 degrees south, deep in the frozen waters of Antarctica's Weddell Sea. The crew of 28 is 100 miles short of their goal, the South Pole. They experience wind speeds of nearly 200

miles an hour and temperatures as low as −100° Fahrenheit.

Investigate

Find latitude 74 degrees south on a map. Find the longitude and latitude of the town in which you live.

Check out this Antarctica Web site: *http://www.theice.org.*

1981

Astronomers at the University of Wisconsin announce the discovery of a star 150,000 light-years away. This star is 3,500 times bigger than the sun.

Figuring out how many miles there are in 150,000 light-years leads to some very big numbers. Nine-year-old Milton Sirotta came up with a name for the number 1 followed by a hundred zeros: *googol*. A googol is more than the number of grains of sand in the world, more than the number of hairs on the heads of all the people in the world. Scientists use powers of ten to work with big numbers. For example, a googol can be written as 10^{100}, $1,000,000 = 10^6$, and $5,000,000 = 5 \times 10^6$.

Investigate

Write some big numbers using exponents: one million, three million, one billion, three billion, one trillion, three trillion.

JANUARY 20

1825

Noah Webster finishes his *American Dictionary of the English Language*. It includes definitions for 70,000 words.

No dictionary can list a whole language. The English language has been estimated at four million words. This includes slang, jargon, dialect, neologisms, medical terms, and the names of registered chemical compounds. The largest American unabridged dictionary,

Webster's Third New International, has 450,000 words. A person typically uses no more than 60,000 words.

Investigate

About how many words are in your classroom dictionaries? Find out without counting every word.

1937

In his inaugural address, President Franklin D. Roosevelt says, "I see one third of a nation ill housed, ill clad, and ill nourished." He institutes such social programs as social security to improve people's lives. Nevertheless, in the 1990s, one in four children in the United States lives below the poverty line.

Investigate

Nationwide, one in four children live in poverty. What is the ratio in your state? How many children is this?

JANUARY 21

1853

Russell Hawes invents an envelope-folding machine; using it, three workers can produce 25,000 envelopes in ten hours.

Investigate

Calculate how many envelopes one person can make in an hour using Hawes's machine.

A standard small envelope for letters measures $6\frac{1}{2}$-by-$3\frac{5}{8}$-inches. Examine an envelope this size and design a paper shape that can be folded to create a similar one. Then undo the original envelope and see how well you did.

1976

A British Airways Concorde leaves London for Bahrain (an island off the coast of Arabia) and an Air France Concorde takes off from Paris to Rio de Janeiro, Brazil, launching the first supersonic regular passenger service. A Concorde jet is 205.7 feet long, has a wingspan of 83.8 feet, weighs 389,000 pounds, reaches a cruising speed of 1,354 miles per hour, holds 100 passengers, can fly 3,970 miles without refueling, and can go as high as 60,000 feet.

The Concorde Web site contains fascinating information about its history: *http://www.concorde-jet.com*.

Investigate

Compare the Concorde's statistics with those of other planes. Is the Concorde's ratio of length to wingspan different from that of other planes? How about its weight?

JANUARY 22

1673

The first U.S. postal route—once-a-month delivery between New York City and Boston—begins operations. Today, 63.5 billion pieces of bulk mail and 13.6 billion catalogs are delivered by the postal service each year, which amounts to an annual average of more than 300 pieces of "junk" mail per person! The U.S. Postal Service owns 182,533 cars and trucks. It is the world's largest civilian fleet of vehicles.

Investigate

Invite a postal worker to talk to your class. Find out how many postal routes there are in your city and how the mail gets sorted.

Keep track of your household junk mail for one week. How many pieces of junk mail arrive? How much do they weigh all together?

1970

The Boeing 747, the world's biggest airplane (nicknamed the Jumbo Jet), making its first commercial flight, lands at Heathrow Airport with 362 passengers on board. This airplane cost $21,400,000 to develop. Today, it can carry more than 400 passengers, has a cruising speed of almost 600 miles (almost 1,000 kilometers) per hour, can fly more than 7,000 miles (more than 11,000 kilometers) without refueling, can ascend to 45,000 feet (13,720 meters), is about 231 feet (about 70 meters) long, has a wingspan of 213 feet (64.9 meters), weighs 710,000 pounds (322,050 kilograms), and is configured with 50 to 60 rows of seats.

Check out these related Web sites: *http://aerofiles.com/chrono.html* and *http://aerofiles.com/aircraft.html*.

Investigate

A Boeing 727 can seat about 145 passengers in 25 rows of seats. If a passenger wants a window seat, will she have a better chance getting one on a 727 or a 747? Present a convincing argument to support your opinion.

JANUARY 23

1849

Elizabeth Blackwell, who had been turned down by 28 colleges before she found one that would let her study medicine, graduates from Geneva Medical College (now Hobart and Williams Smith Colleges) in Geneva, New York, at the head of her class and becomes the first woman doctor in the United States.

For more information about Elizabeth Blackwell, check *http://www.greatwomen.org/blkwele.htm*.

Investigate

Look at the list of doctors in the yellow pages of the phone book. How many are male and how many are female? Can you determine whether female doctors are more apt to specialize in one field of medicine over another?

1985

The Coca-Cola Company announces it is replacing its 99-year-old recipe with a new formula. Customers react so negatively that on July 10 the same year it reintroduces the old Coke under a new name, Coca-Cola Classic.

Investigate

Every minute, people around the world drink 311,111 Cokes. How many Cokes are consumed in one week?

JANUARY 24

1736

The French mathematician Joseph Louis Lagrange is born. He is the youngest of eleven children and the only one to survive past early childhood. Lagrange becomes famous for his work in calculus and the metric system. Until the late 18th century, nearly every district in France (and in other countries) has its own measuring system. This makes it very difficult for people to conduct business. Joseph Lagrange heads the Committee on Weights and Measures, persuading people to adopt a plan using a decimal system. The committee decides that a meter should equal one ten-millionth the distance from the North Pole to the equator. They also decide that a gram equals the weight of one cubic centimeter of distilled water at four degrees centigrade. The metric system is soon adopted throughout Europe. The U.S Metric Association's Web site is *http://lamar.colostate.edu/~hillger/everyday.htm*.

Investigate

A centimeter is about the same as the width as your pinky finger or a button on your shirt. Measure five things in centimeters. Then estimate your own height in centimeters and verify how accurate your estimate was.

1800

Congress approves the purchase of books to start the Library of Congress. Thomas Jefferson's 6,500-volume library is purchased in 1815 and forms the nucleus of the collection. By 1987, the buildings of the Library of Congress cover 64.6 acres of floor space and contain 532 miles of book shelves that hold 22 million books as well as over 60 million other items. Every day, taxpayers spend about $1.2 million dollars on the Library of Congress. On an average workday, the Library of Congress catalogues 730 books, and the Congressional Research Service Office responds to 2,000 research requests. The Library's Web site is *http://lcweb.loc.gov.*

Investigate
Figure out a way to estimate the number of books in your classroom or school library without counting every volume. How does the number compare with the number in Jefferson's personal library?

1915

Alexander Graham Bell places the first long-distance telephone call from New York to San Francisco. The call takes 23 minutes to go through and costs $20.70. By the 1990s, Americans are making 170,579 overseas calls every hour.

Check out the Bell collection at the Library of Congress: *http://lcweb.loc.gov.*

Investigate
Bring in a phone bill for a class math investigation. (Be sure you have parental consent.) What is the average number of long-distance calls made by your household? What is your average length of long-distance calls? What is the average price per minute? Can you learn any other data from these bills?

New York to San Francisco

+ = $20.70

1915

1989

Chicago Bulls star Michael Jordan scores his 10,000th point. It has taken Jordan 303 games to reach this watershed. Wilt Chamberlain did it in 236 games.

The official cyberspace site of the National Basketball Association has lots of other statistics. Check it out at *http://www.nba.com*.

Investigate

What are Jordan's and Chamberlain's respective average points per game? What other statistical comparisons might you come up with for these two stars?

Is there a current basketball great whom you think will top both Chamberlain and Jordan? Research statistics to explain your prediction.

JANUARY 26

1837

Michigan becomes the 26th state admitted to the Union.

To see all the official U.S. flags, go to: *http://www.usflag.org/toc.flags.html*.

Investigate

Create a design with 26 stars that could be used on a U.S. flag. How is this easier or more difficult than creating a flag with 25 or 27 stars?

1875

George Green of Kalamazoo, Michigan, patents the first electric dental drill.

Investigate

Calculate the total number of teeth the students in your class have lost. What's the typical amount of money the tooth fairy leaves per tooth?

JANUARY 27

1854

A clipper ship from San Francisco, carrying a ten-foot-high hollowed-out section of a giant California redwood tree, arrives in Philadelphia. The tree from which the section was taken was 3,000 years old, 325 feet tall, and 90 feet in circumference. A redwood tree's root system is shallow—only between four and six feet deep—but the roots grow out laterally to between $\frac{1}{3}$ and $\frac{1}{2}$ the height of the tree.

Investigate

Make a poster showing a 325-feet-tall redwood tree next to other famous objects such as a tyrannosaurus rex, the Great Pyramids, the Statue of Liberty, or the (Chicago) Sears Tower.

1910

Thomas Crapper dies. He is said to have developed the flush toilet. A flush toilet today uses five to seven gallons of water with each flush. In the United States 4.8 billion gallons of water are used to flush toilets every day.

Investigate

How much water does your family use to flush the toilet each day? How much water does your school use?

JANUARY 28

1841

Henry Morton Stanley is born in Wales. He later becomes the leader of an African expedition to find the missing missionary-explorer David Livingstone, who has not been heard from for more than two years. Stanley begins his search in Africa on

Kansas
January 29, 1861

March 21, 1871; he finds Livingstone, who insists he isn't lost, near Lake Tanganyika on November 10, 1871.

Investigate
How many days did Stanley search for Livingstone?

1878

In New Haven, Connecticut, the first commercial telephone switchboard in the United States opens. It has 21 subscribers. People in the United States now average 1,837 phone calls per person each year.

Investigate
Figure the average number of telephone calls a person makes in one day. Estimate the number of phone subscribers there are in your town. Make your estimate without counting every listing in the phone book, and be prepared to explain the method you used.

1861

Kansas becomes the 34th state. The name *Kansas* comes from an Indian word meaning flat or spreading water. The state flower is the sunflower. The sunflower provides pioneer settlers in the Midwest with oil for their lamps and food for themselves and their stock. Native Americans roast sunflower seeds and ground them into flour for bread or pound them to release an oil for cooking and for making body paint.

Investigate
Look at a live sunflower or a detailed picture of one. A sunflower has two distinct parallel rows of seeds spiraling clockwise and counterclockwise. The seeds are Fibonacci numbers, typically 34 going one way and 55 going the other way, although sometimes they are 55 and 89. Find other natural examples of Fibonacci patterns. Good places to look include pinecones, pineapples, artichokes, and African daisies. For a terrific site on Fibonacci numbers, go

to *http://www.ee.surrey.ac.uk/Personal/R.Knott/Fibonacci/fibnat.html*.

1998

Carl Gorman, a gentle Navajo artist and one of the 400 Navajo code talkers during World War II, dies. Gorman and 28 other Navajo volunteers turned their native language into a secret code that allowed Marine commanders to issue reports and orders and to coordinate complex operations. Although the highly respected Japanese code crackers broke U.S. Army, Navy, and Air Corps codes, they were never able to break the Marine Navajo code. As Gorman's *New York Times* obituary notes, "Navajo is a language without an alphabet and with such a complex, irregular syntax that in 1942 it was estimated that outside of the 50,000 Navajos, no more than 30 other people in the world had any knowledge of it, none of them Japanese." Online information from the Native American museum that is part of the Smithsonian Institution is available at *http://www.si.edu/nmai/nav.htm*. The Navajo Code Talkers' Dictionary is available online at *http://www.history.navy.mil/faqs/faq61-4.htm*.

Investigate
Team up with at least one other person and invent a code using numbers.

JANUARY 30

1946

The first Roosevelt dime is issued. The dime is a particularly suitable coin with which to honor the late president Franklin Delano Roosevelt, who was born on January 30, 1882. In 1937, President Roosevelt, himself crippled by polio, asked each American to send him a dime for polio research. He called this fund-raising campaign the March of Dimes. He received 150,000 letters, each containing a dime. Ten years after

Roosevelt's death, Dr. Jonas Salk announced his discovery of the first polio vaccine.

Investigate
Mental Math: How much money did President Roosevelt receive?

Which is worth more—a dime for every pound you weigh, or a dime for every inch of your height?

1958

The first two-way moving sidewalk was put in service at Love Field airport in Dallas, Texas. The length of the walkway through the airport was 1,435 feet.

Investigate
Mental Math: A mile is 5,280 feet. What fraction of a mile was the moving sidewalk in Love Field?

How many classroom lengths do you think equal 1,435 feet? Estimate and then figure.

JANUARY 31

1961

A 37-pound chimpanzee named Ham, dressed in a space suit and diapers and strapped into a seat at the top of a rocket, is fired 150 miles (241 kilometers) into space. Scientists want to test the effect on primates of the gravitational stresses of ascending from and descending into the Earth's atmosphere. When Ham returns to Earth, he is given lettuce, an apple, and half an orange. Ham retires from the Air Force in 1963 and goes to live at the National Zoo in Washington, D.C. In 1981 he is living at a zoo in North Carolina, where he dies in 1983.

Investigate
Mental Math: How long does Ham live after his historic flight?

1990

More than 30,000 Russians visit the first McDonald's in Moscow on opening day. A Big Mac, fries, and a soft drink cost the equivalent of $9.30. The restaurant seats 700 people and is the largest of the more than 12,000 McDonald's restaurants worldwide. In 1997 the McDonald's Corporation reports that five of their ten busiest franchises in the world are in Russia or Hong Kong.

Investigate

How much does a Big Mac, fries, and a soft drink cost in the United States? If someone earns the minimum wage for an eight-hour workday, a meal at McDonald's uses up what fraction of his or her daily salary?

How many four-item meal combinations can you create from the following, taking one item from each column?

| Big Mac | fries | soda | pie |
| Chicken McNuggets | salad | milkshake | cookie |

What happens if you add a fifth two-item column? a third item to each of the four existing columns?

F E B R U A R Y

FEBRUARY 1

1922

T*he Readers' Digest* magazine is launched. It is now published in 19 languages and reaches 100 million readers around the world each month.

Investigate
Mental Math: How many years has T*he Readers' Digest* been on the newsstands?

Analyze the opening paragraph of a number of *Readers' Digest* articles. Classify types of opening sentences, number of words in a sentence, number of sentences in a paragraph.

1944

Dutch artist Piet Mondrian, born in 1872, dies. Although his father wanted him to follow in his footsteps as a schoolteacher, Mondrian was finally allowed to attend the Academy of Fine Arts in Amsterdam.

Investigate
Look at prints or photographs of some of Mondrian's work and explain why he is called "the painter of geometry."

Create a painting in the style of Mondrian.

FEBRUARY 2

1863

Samuel Langhorne Clemens used the pseudonym of Mark Twain for the first time. On riverboats, one member of the crew always stood near the railing and measured the depth of the water with a long cord with flags spaced a fathom (six feet) apart. When the flags disappeared, the crew member would call out "Mark One!" for one fathom, and for two fathoms he called out "Mark Twain!" Two fathoms meant safe clearance for riverboats.

Investigate
Mental Math: Samuel Clemens was born in 1835. How old was he when he started to call himself Mark Twain?

Mental Math: Mark Twain died in 1910. Had he used the pseudonym for more or less than half his life? Explain your reasoning.

A fathom is a measure of length used for marine depths. List other measures of length and what they're used to measure.

1909

President Theodore Roosevelt makes a list of birds he sees in the vicinity of the White House. He spots 57 varieties. Nine varieties have nests on the White House grounds: woodpeckers, flickers, orioles, purple grackles, redstarts, catbirds, tufted titmice, wood thrushes, and robins.

Investigate
Establish a bird-watching post in your classroom or in your school and enter your "sightings" in a log. At the end of the week, graph the results.

FEBRUARY 3
1984

At Madison Square Garden in New York City, Carl Lewis beats his own world record in the long jump by 9.25 inches. Lewis is regarded by many as the "Greatest Olympian Ever." He won nine Olympic gold medals, winning the gold medal for long jumps in four consecutive Olympics in 1984 (28 feet, 0.25 inches), 1988 (28 feet, 7.5 inches), 1992 (28 feet, 5.5 inches), and 1996 (27 feet, 10.75 inches).

Investigate
What's the difference in length between Carl Lewis's shortest and longest Olympic gold medal long jumps?

Organize a long jump competition and see who jumps the longest and how far.

1992

After signing a five-year, 29-million-dollar contract, Bobby Bonilla of the New York Mets pledges to donate $500 to New York City schools for every run he drives in during the 1992 season.

Investigate
Bonilla drives in 70 runs in 1992, which is down from the 120 he hit in 1990. How much money does he pay the schools?

What percent of Bonilla's five-year income does his gift represent?

FEBRUARY 4
1902

Charles Lindbergh is born. Most people know Lindbergh for his aviation exploits. It is less well known that when Lindbergh is 11 his father teaches him to drive. When Lindbergh is 14, he drives his mother and uncle to California, a trip of 1,600 miles. It takes them 40 days.

Investigate
Figure out how many miles the Lindbergh family averages a day during their 1916 trip. (Obviously, they aren't in a hurry.)

1902

Charles Lindbergh is born.

Using road maps, plan your own 1,600-mile trip. How long do you think the trip will take? Reminder: maps are easily available online.

Research the legal driving age in all 50 states, and make a graph to display the data.

1955

Viking 12, the last in the series of Viking research rockets, lifts off from the White Sands Proving Ground, in New Mexico. A U.S. Navy project, this is the first large rocket designed and built in the United States. It is capable of carrying instruments to altitudes above 1,000,000 feet (305,000 meters). The rocket is 497 inches (12.6 meters) long and weighs 14,815 pounds (6,720 kilograms).

Investigate
How many miles are there in 1,000,000 feet?

Is the weight of all the children in your school, added together, more or less than 14,815 pounds?

FEBRUARY 5

1936

The National Wildlife Federation is founded. It maintains a Web site for kids: *http://www.nwf.org/kids*.

Investigate
Find out which, if any, wild animals are on the endangered list in your state and in neighboring states.

Invite someone from a nearby university cooperative extension or Sierra Club chapter to talk about the numbers involved in declaring an animal endangered.

1954

The first Wiffle ball—a polyethylene baseball—is sold. David Mullany makes this ball for children who don't have access to large open areas. Because it is filled with holes, it can't be thrown or hit far and thus is ideal for street-corner games. Mullany thinks the slang term for missing a pitched baseball—*whiff*—well describes his perforated plastic ball.

The manufacturer's site provides rules of the game and dimensions of a Wiffle field: *http://www.wiffle.com*.

Investigate
Measure and compare the distances you and your classmates can throw a regular baseball and a Wiffle ball. (Make at least five throws with each and find the average distance.)

FEBRUARY 6

1778

France becomes the first nation to recognize the independence of the United States by signing a Treaty of Amity and Commerce and a Treaty of Alliance. Benjamin Franklin represents the United States in the negotiations.

Investigate
Mental Math: How long ago were these treaties signed?

1895

George Herman ("Babe") Ruth is born. The official site of Major League baseball contains Ruth information in its history section—all century team: *http://www.majorleaguebaseball.com*.

Investigate
Research runs-batted-in and similar statistics for the Babe, and compare them with the statistics of some current players.

FEBRUARY 7

1943

To aid the World War II effort, the United States imposes a ration on shoes. Each civilian is limited to three pairs of leather shoes a year.

Investigate
Count the number of pairs of shoes in your closet. Total the number of pairs owned by the class.

How many shoes would be in the classroom if everyone brought in three pairs?

1984

Astronaut Bruce McCandless makes the first unattached (no safety cords!) space walk in history. He floats in space more than 300 feet from the *Challenger* space shuttle.

Investigate
Mark off 100 feet from a given spot; then estimate another 100 feet, and another. Think about how it would feel to float "free" in space that distance from the security of the space ship without a safety cord.

McCandless's walk lasts 5 hours, 55 minutes. An overview and history of space shuttle missions, with fact sheets on specific missions, is available at *http://www.kipertek.com/spaceline/shuttlechron.html*.

FEBRUARY 8

1852

Henry David Thoreau notes in his journal that his neighbor Mrs. Buttrick charges five dollars to make a shirt and that she can make one shirt in a day.

Investigate
How much might Mrs. Buttrick earn a year making shirts?

1994

Kudzu, child of Willie B and Choomba, an African western lowland gorilla couple, is born in the Ford African Rain Forest at the Atlanta Zoo. Willie was born in 1958. Check out the gorilla section of the National Zoological Park's Web site by logging on to *http://natzoo.si.edu*.

Investigate
Mental Math: How old is Willie when his offspring is born?

Why do you think people are so interested in gorillas?

FEBRUARY 9

1824

Two days after his 12th birthday, Charles Dickens starts work at a boot-polish factory. He works from 8 A.M. until 8 P.M. cutting labels and pasting them on shoe-polish pots. Years later Dickens recalls this day: "No words can express the agony of my soul." The rest of his family is shut up in debtors' prison, and Charles visits them once a week. Dickens writes about this painful boyhood experience in such novels as *Oliver Twist* and *David Copperfield*.

There are numerous Web sites about child labor around the world.

Investigate
Mental Math: What year was Charles Dickens born?

1870

The United States Weather Bureau is authorized by Congress. We think people always sat around and talked about the weather, but it took an act of Congress to do something about it! The weather bureau is

officially known as the National Weather Service (NWS) and is a department of the National Oceanic and Atmospheric Administration (NOAA). Check out *http://www.noaa.gov*.

Investigate
Keep a classroom weather chart for thirty days, marking down the temperature when you arrive and leave each day. At the end of the time, write a weather report describing the month's classroom temperatures.

FEBRUARY 10

1863

Alanson Crane, of Fortress Monroe, Virginia, obtains patent number 37,610, for the fire extinguisher.

Investigate
Map the route by which you are to exit the school building from your classroom in case of a fire.

Map the fire exit route from the cafeteria; from the library.

1934

The U.S. Postal Service issues the first sheets of postage stamps in New York City. They are unperforated and ungummed sheets, requiring people to cut the stamps out of the sheet and then put some glue on the back to get them to stick on an envelope. The Postal Service changed this after many complaints.

Investigate
How many first-class stamps come on a sheet today? How much does a sheet cost?

1863
Fortress Monroe, Virginia

PATENT
37,610

1ˢᵗ

FEBRUARY 11

660 B.C.

According to tradition, this is the day Japan's first emperor ascends the throne, marking the country's beginning. The day is recognized as Japan Founding Day

Investigate
Celebrate the day by practicing one of Japan's ancient arts: origami, the art of paper folding. You can get some online advice at *http://www.origami-usa.org*.

Mental Math: How long ago was Japan founded?

1929

Time magazine reports the death of William Cullen Bryant ("Doc") Kemp, age 78. He is known as the perpetual student of Columbia University, having earned the following degrees: B.A., M.A., M.D., L.L.M., L.L.B., Ph.D., C.E., E.E., Mech. E., E.M. Pharm. Chem., B.S. When Kemp was a lazy freshman at Columbia, his relatives promised him $2,500 for each year he studied at the university. He stayed 60 years.

Investigate
Mental Math: What year was William Cullen Bryant Kemp born?

How much money did Kemp receive by staying in school? Do you think this was a good deal?

FEBRUARY 12

1879

The first indoor ice-skating rink opens at Madison Square Garden, in New York City. The surface of the ice is 6,000 square feet.

Investigate
What is the area of your classroom floor?

What is the area of the floor of the largest room in your school?

1992

Tenants of the Lincoln Building, a 55-story office tower on Forty-Second Street in New York City, invite 7,500 guests from neighboring offices to a Lincoln party, complete with a birthday cake with 183 candles. Singers from the Manhattan Opera Association perform President Lincoln's favorite songs, including "Annie Laurie," "Yankee Doodle," and "Dixie."

   This Lincoln site, created by a history teacher, contains lots of information: *http://home.att.net/~rjnorton/Lincoln77.html*.

Investigate
Mental Math: What year was President Lincoln born?

Mental Math: How many candles will a Lincoln birthday cake need today?

Convert a standard cake recipe into one for a cake that will be large enough for the class, and then for a cake that will be large enough for 7,500 guests.

FEBRUARY 13

1635

The Public Latin School for boys is organized in Boston. It has been in continuous existence ever since and is the oldest public school in America. At its

inception, it trained students for the ministry, helping them "obtain a knowledge of the Scriptures." The school was originally supported by voluntary contributions.

Investigate
Mental Math: How old is the Boston Latin School?

When was your school built? How old is it?

1939

Louis Brandeis retires from the Supreme Court, at age 82. Appointed in January 1916 by Woodrow Wilson, Brandeis is acknowledged to be one of America's greatest legal minds.

   Information on current justices is available at *http://oyez.nwu.edu*. The site also provides searches for former justices.

Investigate
How old was Brandeis when he was appointed to the Supreme Court?

What is the average age at which a judge is appointed to the Supreme Court?

FEBRUARY 14

1848

Emily Dickinson, now regarded as one of our foremost poets, writes to her brother from Mount Holyoke Seminary, "Mistress Lyon arose in the hall and forbade our sending 'any of those foolish notes called Valentines.'" Americans now send more than one billion Valentines each year.

Investigate
If everybody in your class gives everybody else a Valentine, how many Valentines is that altogether?

February 14, 1848

1946

The U.S. War Department announces the invention of a machine that applies electronic speed to mathematical tasks. They call it ENIAC—Electronic Numerical Integrator and Computer. This computer is huge, covering fifteen thousand square feet of the basement of the Moore School of Electronic Engineering, at the University of Pennsylvania in Philadelphia. Computers are a lot smaller these days.

Investigate
Mental Math: How old would this computer be today?

How much floor or desk area space does a personal computer take up today?

FEBRUARY 15

1842

The City Despatch [sic] Post Office, in New York City, uses adhesive postage stamps for the first time. The 3-cent stamps are printed in sheets of 42; the discounted price for one hundred stamps is $2.50.

Investigate
How much would someone in 1842 save if he bought 504 stamps all at once instead of buying a sheet of 42 stamps every week for 12 weeks?

1971

Great Britain converts to the metric system, leaving the United States as the only large industrial nation not using this standard system of measurement. The Web site of the U.S. Metric Association is *http://lamar.colostate .edu/~hillger/everyday.htm*.

Investigate
What are the merits of metric measurement?

How tall are you in centimeters? Make a graph of the heights of all the students in your class.

FEBRUARY 16
1923

A *New York Times* headline calls this the most extraordinary day in the history of Egyptian excavation. It is the day Tu-Ankh-amen's tomb is opened, revealing splendors untouched for 3,400 years. You can look at the beautiful Egyptian artifacts housed in the Institute of Egyptian Art and Archaeology by logging on to *http://www .memphis.edu/egypt/artifact.html*.

Investigate
How would a year 3,400 years ago be recorded?

1993

Geoff Case races up the 1,575 steps of New York's Empire State Building in 10 minutes and 18 seconds. The previous record had been set in 1988 by Australian Craig Logan, who did it in 11 minutes and 29 seconds.
   The Empire State Building Web site contains interesting information: *http://www .esbnyc.com*.

Investigate
How much time does Case average on each step?

By how much does Case beat Logan's time?

FEBRUARY 17
1859

West Point Cadet George Custer receives three demerits for throwing snowballs. During his four-year stay at West Point, Custer, who later becomes General Custer, accumulates 726 demerits.

Investigate
If he received the same number of demerits each year, how many demerits does Custer accumulate each year he spends at West Point?

1982

At the American Toy Fair, in New York City, toy makers introduce Jelly Belly dolls. There are three varieties. One smells like bubble gum, one smells like lemon drops, and one smells like purple punch.

Investigate
What are the most popular toys this year? Graph the top contenders.

FEBRUARY 18
1745

Count Alessandro Volta, future Italian physicist and inventor of the electric battery, is born. You can find a brief description of his battery experiment at *http://www.letsfindout.com /subjects/science/alessandro-volta.html*.

Investigate
What would life be like without batteries? For one thing, there would be no remote controls. How many things in your home require batteries?

1908

U.S. postage stamps were sold for the very first time. They cost only a penny. Postal rates have changed many times since 1908. It cost 3 cents to mail a letter in 1917, 4 cents in 1958, 5 cents in 1963, 10 cents in 1974, 22 cents in 1985, 29 cents in 1991, 32 cents in 1995, and 33 cents in 1999.

Investigate
What percent increase has there been in first-class postage rates in the last ten years?

What do you predict the postage will be for a letter in the year 2010? Explain your reasoning.

FEBRUARY 19

1878

Thomas Alva Edison, of Menlo Park, New Jersey, receives patent number 200,521, for a "phonograph or speaking machine." The first recorded sound is Edison reciting "Mary had a little lamb." You can find out more about this and other Edison inventions at *http://homestead.juno.com/pdeisch/files/edison.htm.*

Investigate
Mental Math: How long ago did Edison begin attempting to record sound?

Conduct a poll: How much time a day do your classmates spend listening to CDs or tapes?

1992

Gamma, a chimpanzee, dies at the Yerkes Primate Research Center, in Atlanta, Georgia. At 59 years 5 months, Gamma is the oldest known nonhuman primate.

Investigate
Mental Math: In what month and year was Gamma born?

Using almanacs and encyclopedias, find out the lifespan of other living things. Find a way to display this information.

FEBRUARY 20

1872

Silas Noble and James Cooley, of Granville, Massachusetts, receive a patent for a machine to manufacture toothpicks.

Investigate
Mental Math: How long has the lowly toothpick been a patented product?

1962

Astronaut John Glenn becomes the first American to orbit the Earth. Once he reaches orbit, Glenn travels at 17,545 miles per hour. His peak altitude is 162.3 miles. The circumference of the Earth is 24,000 miles.

Investigate
About how long does it take Glenn to make a single orbit of the Earth?

Find some interesting numerical comparisons with the altitude Glenn reaches. For example, how high is 162 miles in terms of things on Earth?

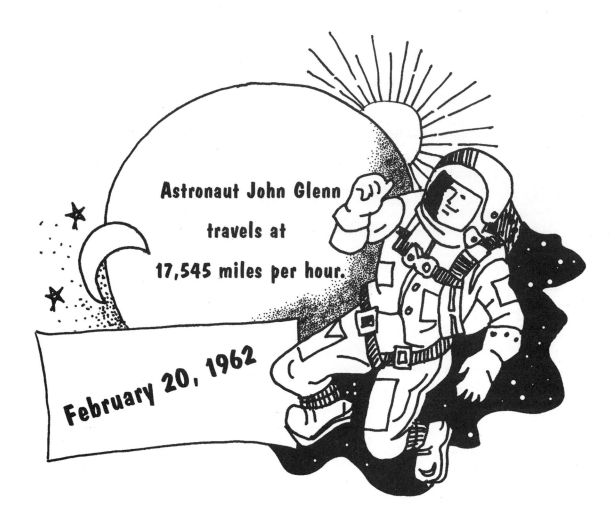

Astronaut John Glenn travels at 17,545 miles per hour.

February 20, 1962

FEBRUARY 21

1853

Congress authorizes the minting of three-dollar gold coins. Mints stop making these coins in September 1890.

The U.S. Mint provides interesting information on the Sacagawea Golden Dollar: *http://www.usmint.gov*.

Investigate
Mental Math: For how many years are these coins minted?

Write an essay arguing why a three-dollar coin would or would not be a good idea today.

1866

Lucy B. Hobbs graduates from the Ohio College of Dental Surgery, in Cincinnati, Ohio. She is the first woman to obtain a D.D.S. degree.

Investigate
Mental Math: How many years ago did Lucy graduate from dental school?

What fraction or percentage of the dentists listed in your city's yellow pages are women?

FEBRUARY 22

1784

The Empress of China, a 360-ton trading ship, leaves New York. It arrives in Canton, China, on August 28, 1784, leaves China for the return voyage on December 28, 1784, and arrives back in New York on May 11, 1785.

How long did each segment of the round-trip take?

Why do you think the return voyage was so much shorter than the outbound voyage?

1881

An obelisk measuring 90 feet high and weighing 443,000 pounds, built in Heliopolis, Egypt between 1591 and 1565 B.C. and removed to Alexandria in 22 B.C., is officially presented to the City of New York, a gift from the Khedive of Egypt. When the obelisk is shipped to the United States, a hole has to be cut in the starboard bow of the boat.

Nova covers a modern attempt to raise an obelisk using only ancient tools: *http://www.pbs.org/wgbh/nova/egypt/raising.*

Investigate
Mental Math: How old is this obelisk now?

Do you think the weight of all the students in your school, added together, would equal the weight of the obelisk?

FEBRUARY 23
1886

Charles Martin Hall finalizes a process for making aluminum electrically rather than chemically, thereby greatly reducing its cost.

Investigate
Estimate how many aluminum cans are in each class member's home. Have each student check and report back the next day.

February 23, 1978

1978

Professional basketball player Clifford Ray saves the life of a bottle-nosed dolphin at Marine World USA, in California. The dolphin has swallowed a three-inch bolt accidentally left in its tank. A veterinarian tries to remove the bolt from the dolphin's stomach, but he can't reach it. Clifford Ray volunteers to try. He cuts his fingernails, greases his arm (which is three feet, nine inches long), reaches down through the dolphin's mouth, grabs the bolt, and extracts it.

Investigate

In pairs, measure each other's arms. List the measurements from smallest to largest. How do the lengths of students' arms compare with the length of Ray's arm?

FEBRUARY 24

1949

At the White Sands Proving Ground, in New Mexico, a two-stage rocket is fired about 250 miles into space at an approximate speed of 5,000 miles an hour.

Investigate

About how long did it take for the rocket to travel 250 miles?

1924

Johnny "Tarzan" Weissmuller broke the world's record in the 100-meter swimming event. He did it in $57\frac{2}{5}$ seconds.

Investigate

Research the fastest time on record today for swimming 100 meters. How much faster is it than Johnny Weissmuller's time?

FEBRUARY 25

1905

Adelle Davis, future nutritionist and author, is born. Later, her fervent message is, "You are what you eat!" Information on the food pyramid can be obtained online at *http://vm.cfsan.fda.gov/label.html* and *www.nal.usda.gov/fnic/foodcomp*. Science in the Public Interest publishes items of nutritional interest online at *www.cspinet.org*.

Investigate

Keep a food diary for a week, carefully writing down everything you eat. Categorize these foods according to the food pyramid.

Draw a self-portrait showing your nutrition for the week.

1919

Oregon becomes the first state to tax gasoline; the tax is one cent per gallon.

Investigate

Examine a gas pump at a gas station; how much of the cost of a gallon of gas is tax? How much tax would you pay if you needed twenty gallons to fill your tank?

FEBRUARY 26

1909

The American Bowling Congress awards the first gold medals for perfect-score games.

Investigate

Explore the mathematics of keeping score in bowling.

1919

Two national parks are established. The Grand Canyon National Park, in northwest Arizona, covers 1,218,375 acres. Acadia National Park, on Mount Desert Island, near Bar Harbor, Maine, covers 27,871 acres.

Investigate

How far apart are these two national parks? How long do you think it would take to travel between the two?

FEBRUARY 27

1964

The Italian government announces that it is reviewing suggestions from around the world to save the Leaning Tower of Pisa from collapse. It has been shifting since construction started in 1173 on the first three stories. Because it was built on soft ground, the tower started tilting immediately. One hundred years later, four more stories and a bell tower were added, at a slight angle, in hopes of correcting the tilt. The 8-story circular tower is 55 meters (180 feet) tall and 16 meters (52 feet) in diameter at the base. A 294-step interior spiral staircase leads to the bell tower. Currently, the tower tilts 5 meters (16 feet) from the vertical, increasing about 1 millimeter ($\frac{1}{25}$ an inch) per year.

Investigate
Bring in cylindrical containers: cans, cereal boxes, and so on, and investigate the base diameter/height ratio.

1988

U. S. speed skater Bonnie Blair wins the Olympics 500 meter speed skating event in a record time of 39.1 seconds. At the 1994 Olympics in Lillehammer, Norway, Bonnie brings her total of gold medals to five, making her the most successful U. S. female athlete in the history of winter Olympics.

Investigate
Research the speed athletes reach in different sports: track and field, skiing, swimming, and so on. Graph the results.

FEBRUARY 28

1940

The first basketball games to be televised are played in Madison Square Garden and telecast over Station W2XBS. Fordham University loses to the University of Pittsburgh, 37 to 50, and Georgetown loses to New York University, 27 to 50.

Investigate
Compare these score totals with those of current college games. How do they compare with current professional game totals? How do you account for this?

1983

One hundred and twenty-five million viewers tune into the last episode of M*A*S*H, the largest audience for a regular TV show in TV history. In the eleven years it played in prime time, 251 episodes were aired. Today, 66 percent of U.S. homes have three or more TV sets, and the average child sees twenty thousand thirty-second commercials a year.

Investigate
How many TV sets are in your home? What's the average number of TV sets per home if you include everyone in your class?

How many hours of TV watching do those twenty thousand commercials represent?

M A R C H

1872

Congress establishes Yellowstone National Park "for the enjoyment of the public." The area is originally 3,348 square miles. It now consists of a total of 2,213,205 acres in three states: Wyoming, Montana, and Idaho.

Investigate
Prepare a map of national parks, indicating the approximate size of each. Then estimate how long it would take to get to the park you'd most like to visit.

1912

Albert Berry makes the first parachute jump. Jumping from a biplane 1,500 feet (457 meters) over Jefferson Barracks, in central Missouri, Berry falls 400 feet (122 meters) before his parachute opens and he lands safely. Today, Don Kellner holds the record for the most parachute jumps—22,750 and counting. His wife flies the plane he jumps from.

Investigate
Mental Math: How long ago was the first parachute jump made?

If Kellner has been jumping for 20 years, about how many jumps is he averaging each week if he jumps on a regular schedule?

MARCH 2

1889

Congress establishes the National Zoological Park, in Washington, D.C. You can visit the National Zoological Park online at *http://www.si.edu*.

Investigate
Take a class poll: What is the favorite zoo animal? Come up with a way to display the poll results.

1987

Benjamin Barreaux, age 11, wins $500 from his mother for not watching television for a year. You may want to check out TV Free America, an organization devoted to reducing children's TV viewing. The Web site is *www.tvturnoff.org*.

Investigate
Take a class poll: What is the peak day and hour students in your class watch TV?

Figure out how many hours of television you watch in a year. Then make a list of all the things you can do instead of watching television. As a class, list these activities on adding machine tape and see how far the list extends down the school corridors.

What is it worth to you to give up TV for a year?

MARCH 3

1845

Florida is admitted to the Union as the 27th state. By the 1990s 14 million people live in Florida and 44 million tourists visit the state each year. The population is increasing by about 1,000 a day. Every hour almost 20 acres of land are cleared for development. Conservationists say that natural Florida is disappearing at twice the rate the Brazilian rain forest is. On the positive side, Big

Cypress National Preserve and Everglades National Park together occupy two million acres, or 3,125 square miles, an area larger than the state of Delaware.

Investigate
How many acres of Florida land are being cleared a year?

1995

At the World Trade Center in Boston, Iowa State architecture student Bryan Berg builds a house of cards that has 83 stories. Bryan's tower has three cards per side in its bottom stories. The completed structure uses 27,000 cards.

Investigate
There are 52 cards in a standard deck; there are also two jokers. How many decks of cards did Bryan use? (Include the jokers.)

MARCH 4

1877

Future inventor Garrett Morgan is born in Paris, Kentucky, seventh of eleven children. In 1914 Morgan receives patent number 1,113,675, for the "safety hood." Today we call it the gas mask. In 1923, he receives patent number 1,475,024 for another device that saves many lives: the traffic light.

The U.S. Patent and Trademark office provides an interesting kids' page: *http://www.uspto.gov/go/kids*.

Investigate
How many patents were issued between Morgan's first and second patents? About how many a year is that?

1968

The United States launches OGA 5, an orbiting geophysical laboratory that collects data on the Sun's influence on Earth.

Investigate

Research information about the Sun online at *http://www.gsfc.nasa.gov* and *http://pds.jpl.nasa.gov/planets/*.

How far is the Sun from Earth? How do the two bodies compare in size?

MARCH 5

1853

Three Steinweg brothers, ages 21, 20, and 16, recent immigrants to the United States, get tired of working for $7 a week, and open a piano-making business together. They Americanize their name and call it Steinway & Sons. In 1856, Steinway & Sons makes 208 pianos; in 1858, this jumps to 712 pianos, and in 1863, to 1,623 pianos. In 1858 the cheapest piano is $275. By 1863, the cheapest is $500.

For a factory tour showing how a piano is made, visit *http://www.steinway.com*.

Investigate

Mental Math: How long has the Steinway company been making pianos?

Mental Math: Estimate the cost of 712 pianos at $275 and the cost of 1,623 pianos at $500. Which do you think is easier to estimate? Explain your reasoning.

1982

Congress declares an International Day of the Seal to alert people to the cruelty of seal hunts. In the wild, the harbor seal can

grow to a length of eight feet and a weight of 300 pounds or more.

The Marine Mammal Center Web site provides a lot of data on seals: *http://www.tmmc.org*.

Investigate
Would a person eight feet tall weigh more, less, or about 300 pounds? Explain your reasoning.

MARCH 6
1902

The U.S. Census Bureau is created. Today the Census Bureau offers a free Population Resource Package, appropriate for students in grades three through eight. The focus is on national population trends and map-related activities. You can contact the Census Bureau at *www.census.gov*.

Investigate
How might you estimate the number of students in your school without counting every student?

1912

The first Oreo cookies go on sale. According to *The Guinness Book of Records*, the Oreo is now the world's favorite cookie. More than six billion are sold each year. Today at Nabisco factories, 2,000 Oreo cookies a minute come out of ovens as long as football fields. Nabisco offers 26 recipes using Oreo cookies. Check out their Web site: *nabisco.com*.

Investigate
Mental Math: How old is the Oreo cookie?

How high a tower would 2,000 Oreos make?

Would you rather have a number of Oreos equal to your height or your weight?

In 1912, $9\frac{1}{2}$ pounds of Oreos cost $1.85. In 1991, a 20-ounce bag cost $3.19. How much would $9\frac{1}{2}$ pounds cost at 1991 rates?

MARCH 7
1854

Charles Miller, of St. Louis, Missouri, receives a patent on a sewing machine to manufacture buttonholes.

Investigate
Estimate how many buttonholes there are in the classroom. Then verify your estimate.

1955

Peter Pan, with Mary Martin and Cyril Richard, is presented as a television special for the first time.

Investigate
Poll how many of the students in your class have read *Peter Pan*, seen it on television, seen it in a movie theater. Graph the results.

Make a graph of your classmates' favorite characters from *Peter Pan*.

MARCH 8
1911

The New York City Police Department obtains its first conviction based on fingerprints.

Investigate
Make your own thumbprints on an index card. Then come up with a system for classifying the class set.

1994

At 7 P.M., helicopters drop explorer Will Steger, five other people, and thirty-three dogs at the edge of Siberia. Their goal is to cross the ice-covered Arctic Ocean. Each sled carries 1,300 pounds of gear and food. The food includes 50 pounds of caribou meat, 3,600 Carbo-Crunch bars, 450 pounds of cheese, 225 pounds of butter, 200 pounds of noodles, 100 pounds of dried fruit, and 200 pounds of soup mix. Because of the extreme cold and the hard work, each team member eats 5,000 calories a day. They try to drink three quarts of water a day. Each dog eats a special two-pound brick of concentrated food. Each brick contains 6,000 calories.

Investigate
How many glasses are there in three quarts of liquid? How does this compare with the number of glasses of liquid you drink in a day?

Figure out the number of calories you eat in a typical day.

Why do you think these explorers carried so much butter and cheese?

MARCH 9
1822

Charles M. Graham, of New York, receives a patent for artificial teeth.

Investigate
How many teeth are there in your classroom? Estimate and then count.

1943

Bobby Fischer, who will become the first American world chess champion, is born.

For an interesting look at the way chess is pictured on postage stamps around the world, go to *http://www.tri.org.au/chess*.

Investigate
There are 64 squares on a chess board. What attributes can you discover about the number 64?

Teacher's note:

64 is the sixth power of 2: $2 \times 2 \times 2 \times 2 \times 2 \times 2$

64 is the third power of 4: $4 \times 4 \times 4$

64 is a square number: 8×8

$64 = 1 + 3 + 5 + 7 + 9 + 11 + 13 + 15$

64 is a multiple of 2, 4, 8, 16, and 32, as well as of 1 and 64.

MARCH 10
1953

Colonel John Hunt and his Mt. Everest reconnaissance team, including Edmund Hillary of New Zealand, leave Kathmandu. (Thirteen previous expeditions to scale Everest have failed.) Eight tons of supplies have already been hauled by porters to an advance base camp on Everest. Scaling the mountain is so rigorous that the climbers cannot afford to take anything extra. At 29,028 feet (8,848 meters) Mt. Everest is the world's highest mountain. (Olympus Mons, on Mars, is about 86,614 feet, or 26,400 meters, high.)

For a description of how the height of Everest was determined, go to *http://www .m.chiba-u.ac.jp/class/respir/hyoko_e.htm*.

Investigate
Do some research. How does the highest mountain in the United States compare in height with Everest? How many floors would an Everest-high skyscraper have?

1977

The rings of Uranus are discovered.

Investigate
What are some facts about Uranus? Check out the NASA Web site at *http://www.nasa.gov* and *http://pds.jpl.nasa.gov/planets*.

Is Uranus a planet astronauts are likely to visit?

It takes Uranus 84 Earth years to orbit the Sun. How would your life change if it took the Earth this long to orbit the sun? How long would winter be?

MARCH 11

1888

The Great Blizzard of '88 dumps 45 to 50 inches of snow on the Northeast. Wind piles snowdrifts 40 feet high in places.

Investigate
Mental Math: How many feet are 45 inches? 50 inches?

How would a snowdrift 40 feet high compare with your height?

1957

American admiral and polar explorer Richard E. Byrd dies. In his autobiography, *Alone*, he writes, "But among the handful who have actually attained Latitude 90 degrees, whether North or South, I doubt that even one found the sight of the pole itself particularly inspiring. For there is little enough to see: at one end of the earth a mathematical spot in the center of a vast and empty ocean, and at the other end an equally imaginary spot in the middle of a vast and windy plateau. It's not getting to the pole that counts. It's what you learn of scientific value on the way. Plus the fact you get there and back without being killed."

Admiral Byrd's biography, along with a time line, is online at *http://www-bprc.mps .ohio-state.edu*.

Investigate
Why might someone want to go to "a mathematical spot" in the middle of a place where all you can see is snow?

MARCH 12

1904

Industrialist and philanthropist Andrew Carnegie gives New York City $5,200,000 for its library system. With this money 39 branch libraries are built throughout the city. In all, Carnegie pays for the building of nearly 3,000 libraries across the country. (The community has to agree to maintain the library.)

Investigate
Is the library in your town or city a Carnegie library?

What is your school library's yearly budget? About how many books will this amount buy?

1976

The baseball team that will become known as the Toronto Blue Jays receives a franchise. Team owners hold a contest to choose a name, asking Toronto residents to come up with ideas.

Investigate
Take a poll to find out what bird would be good for naming your class. For an online bird guide, check *http://www.enature.com*.

MARCH 13

1986

Susan Butcher wins the 14th Iditarod Trail Sled Dog Race, setting a record time of 11 days, 15 hours, and 6 minutes. This is her first of four Iditarod wins. The race begins in downtown Anchorage, Alaska, and winds 1,049 miles to Nome. The dogs' and drivers' physical condition is monitored at health and safety checkpoints along the way. At one checkpoint dogs and drivers are required to rest for 24 hours.

For a history and lots of current information on the Iditarod, see *http://www.workingdogweb.com/iditarod.htm#history*.

Investigate
A racing sled dog consumes 8,000 calories a day. How does this compare with how many calories you consume a day?

Figure out when Susan Butcher began the race from Anchorage.

1988

The longest recorded conga line, the Miami Super Conga, is formed during Calle Ocho, a party to which Cuban-Americans invite the rest of Miami to celebrate their life together. The conga line is made up of 119,986 people.

Investigate
About how long might this conga line have been? How would you go about finding out? What is best to express the answer—inches, feet, yards, or miles? Explain your reasoning.

MARCH 14

1932

Sixteen bulls and thirteen cows and heifers arrive at the King Ranch, Kingsville, Texas. They left Capetown, South Africa, on November 14, 1931, and were held in quarantine from December 12, 1931, to March 9, 1932, at the U.S. Department of Agriculture, Animal Quarantine Station, Clifton, New Jersey.

Investigate:
On a world map, plot the route the cattle might have followed. How many miles did they travel?

How many days were the cattle in the United States before they finally reached their home?

1995

A national poll rates the top five pets for U.S. families:

Dogs	37%
Cats	31%
Birds	6%
Fish	3%
Horses	3%

Investigate
Take a class pet poll and compare statistics. Then poll the class about pets they'd *like* to have. Do the numbers come out differently?

MARCH 15

44 B.C.

Julius Caesar is assassinated. (March 15 is also know as the Ides of March.)

Investigate
Mental Math: About how long ago did this event occur?

Research who Julius Caesar was.

1937

The first blood bank in America is established in Chicago. There are between five million and six million red blood cells in one drop of blood. There are also between five thousand and ten thousand white blood cells in that same drop of blood.

Investigate
What is the ratio of white to red blood cells, using the five million and five thousand estimates?

MARCH 16

1937

Dr. Amos Tversky, future cognitive psychologist, is born. During his career he investigates how people make decisions. In 1988, he publishes a study, based on his analysis of the National Basketball Association playoffs, that disproves the popular belief that players have "hot hands"—that is, that when a player has just made a shot, he is more likely to make the next attempt.

Investigate
Undertake your own version of another Tversky study. Fill two identical bags with the same number of poker chips or colored tiles. In one bag, place ten chips of one color and two of a second color. In the second bag, reverse the colors. Without looking inside, remove chips from each bag one at a time and try to figure out which bag has which proportion of the two colors. Give reasons for your opinions. Try this again with other proportions of colors, or with three colors in a bag.

1952

Cilaos, on Reunion Island, east of Madagascar, has the rainiest day on record. In 24 hours, 73.62 inches of rain fall.

Investigate
Keep track of the rainfall in your area for the next month. Then compare the total rainfall with just this one day in Madagascar.

Check out an online weather site: *http//www.WHNT19.com/kidwx* is a good one.

MARCH 17

1969

The city of St. Petersburg, Florida, ends its 768-day streak of consecutive sunny days.

Investigate
Keep track of consecutive sunny days for the rest of the year. What's the longest streak you have?

When did St. Petersburg's sunny streak begin?

1989

The remains of the oldest known Egyptian mummy are found near the Great Pyramid of Cheops, in Gia, Egypt. The high-ranking young woman was buried around 2600 B.C.

Investigate
Locate this burial on a time line. Identify other B.C. events.

Visit the Institute of Egyptian Art and Archaeology online at *http://www.memphis .edu/egypt/artifact.html*.

MARCH 18

1748

George Washington visits the first spa open to the public, in Bath, Virginia, now known as Berkeley Springs, West Virginia. The water temperature at this spa is 110 degrees.

Investigate
Prepare several containers of water ranging from "room temperature" to "hot." Measure the exact thermal temperature of each. Where in the sequence would water from this spa fit in?

1944

Since the beginning of World War II, alarm clocks had become precious commodities. Alarm clocks went on sale once again on this day in Chicago, IL.

Investigate
Poll how the students in your class are awakened each morning—by an alarm clock, by another person, in some other way? Graph the results.

An alarm clock riddle: If you go to bed at 8:00 and set the alarm for 9:00, how much sleep will you get? (Answer: If it's a digital clock, probably 13 hours. If it's an analog clock, only 1 hour!)

MARCH 19

1776

The first notice is taken of swallows returning to the old mission of San Juan Capistrano, in California. The swallows stay in Capistrano until March 23, when they leave for Argentina.

Investigate
Consult an atlas and plan a possible route for the swallows. How many miles will they fly?

If you made this journey, how many time zones would you travel through?

1918

Congress passes the Standard Time Act, which establishes standard time zones for the United States.

Investigate
Think about why standard time zones are important. Check out time zones online at *http://tycho.usno.navy.mil/time.html*.

Make up a time zone puzzle. Choose two cities and a time in one of them. Figure out the time in the other. Then give your puzzle to a classmate to solve. For example, if it is 8 A.M. in San Francisco, what time is it in Amsterdam?

MARCH 20

1900

A patent is issued for Nikola Tesla's radio invention. Marconi gets more notice, but his patent application is not filed until November 10 that same year.

For the story of a third-grade class working to get the Smithsonian to give Tesla his due, go to *http://www.concentric.net/~jwwagner/index.shtml*.

Investigate
Poll your classmates to find out the three favorite radio stations, and graph the data.

Invite someone from a local radio station to talk with your class about radio signals.

1926

Mitsumasa Anno, who grows up to write and illustrate children's books, is born. *Anno's Mysterious Multiplying Jar* is a magical depiction of factorial numbers. *Topsy-Turvies: Pictures to Stretch the Imagination*, a book of visual riddles, contains twelve "impossibilities."

Investigate
Read some of Anno's books.

How does Anno construct the visual "impossibilities" in *Topsy-Turvies*?

Find out what "factorial numbers" are.

Explore other optical illusions online at *http://www.illusionworks.com*.

MARCH 21
1685

Organist and composer Johann Sebastian Bach is born. He is one of the most influential composers in musical history.

Investigate
Listen to a piece by Bach. Does anything you hear suggest why he is considered a "mathematical" composer?

1965

Martin Luther King, Jr., leads 3,200 people on a five-day civil rights march from Selma, Alabama, to Montgomery, Alabama.

Investigate
How many miles did the civil rights demonstrators march?

If the demonstrators marched eight abreast, how many rows of marchers were there? What if they marched ten abreast? Twenty?

MARCH 22
1733

Joseph Priestly invents carbonated water, a basic ingredient for soft drinks.

Investigate
Bring in a soda container from home. Examine the ingredients. Some sodas are made with all-natural ingredients, getting their flavor and color and sweetness from different kinds of fruit. Others mix natural and artificial ingredients.

Graph the classwide findings about soda ingredients and nutritional value.

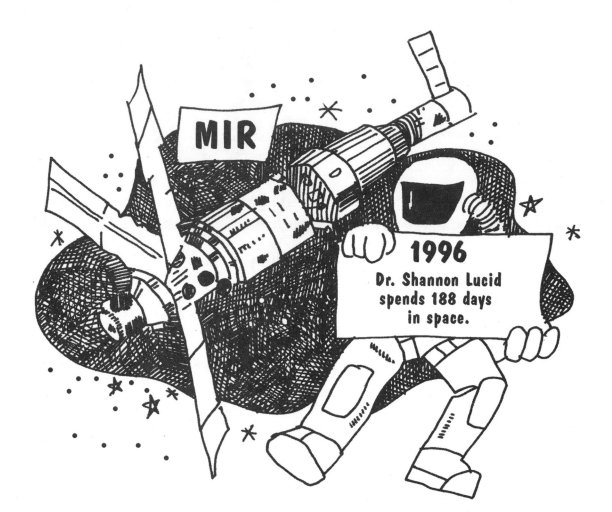

1996

Dr. Shannon Lucid spends 188 days in space.

1996

Astronaut Shannon Lucid is aboard the space shuttle *Atlantic* when it blasts off from Kennedy Space Center. The shuttle docks with Russia's Mir Space Station, and Lucid boards Mir, where she stays for the next 188 days, setting the record for time spent by a woman in space. She also holds the record for the most space flights made by a woman: five.

The Mir Space Station has a Web page, updated frequently: *http://www.maximov.com/Mir/mircurrent.asp*.

Investigate

How many months are there in 188 days?

Gather facts about space travel from the NASA Web site *http://shuttle.nasa.gov*. Create your own shuttle mission log.

MARCH 23

1900

The Waitresses' Union Local 240 of Seattle, Washington, is organized. At that time, women and girls are working eleven and twelve hours a day, seven days a week, for $5.00 a week. The union asks for a ten-hour day and $8.50 a week.

Investigate

How much will an increase of $3.50 per week amount to in a year?

What restrictions are there on how many hours a waitperson can work today?

1910

Trial runs are held on the first automobile speedway at the Los Angeles Motordrome, near Playa del Rey, California. The pie-shaped track is made of wood and has a circumference of 5,281 feet.

Investigate
Research the circumference of today's famous racetracks.

MARCH 24

1874

Harry Houdini, future magician, is born in Budapest, Hungary.

The Houdini Museum has an illustrated Houdini biography: *http://www.microserve.net/~magicusa/houdini.html*.

Investigate
Mental Math: How long ago was Houdini born?

Research Houdini's famous "magic" feats.

1911

The Children's Room of the New York Public Library opens.

Investigate
Devise a plan for estimating how many books are in the school library without counting every volume.

MARCH 25

1514

Pope Leo X receives Hanno, a young white Indian elephant, a gift from the king of Portugal. Every day Hanno drinks 35 to 50 gallons of water and consumes 75 to 100 pounds of fodder, including coconuts, mangoes, plantain stems, root vegetables, oats, and bran.

An elephant can maintain a running speed of about 25 miles (40 kilometers) per hour. In comparison, a female sprinter runs about 21 miles (34 kilometers) per hour.

The Born Free Project provides information on efforts to protect elephants: *http://www.bornfree.org.uk/ele/O.htm*.

Investigate
How many gallons of liquid, in total, do you and your classmates drink a day?

Compare your running speed with that of an elephant.

1933

Explorer Richard Byrd notes a noontime temperature of 64 degrees below zero in his sunless Antarctic base camp. In his diary he mentions trying to warm up the crank case oil in the engines with a blowtorch.

Investigate
Mental Math: Figure out the difference between today's temperature and Byrd's −64 degree weather.

MARCH 26

1819

The charter for the Bank for Savings, in New York City, is granted. The bank starts taking deposits in July. On the first day, eight depositors deposit a total of $2,807.

Investigate
Money in the bank can earn interest. If you put ten dollars in the bank today, find out how much your bank account will have in it at the end of the year.

1936

A telescope lens 200 inches in diameter, which has been molded by the Corning Glass Works in Corning, New York, is shipped to the California Institute of Technology for grinding and polishing before being installed in a telescope at the Mount Polomar Observatory, in San Diego

County. The grinding and polishing takes eleven years.

Investigate

About how many students lying end to end would it take to equal 200 inches?

The lens weighs twenty tons. About how many students does it take to equal this weight?

MARCH 27

1884

The first long-distance telephone call is made by a branch manager of the American Bell Telephone Company in Boston. He calls a branch manager in New York City.

Investigate

Study your parents' phone bill and figure out the longest distance called.

1952

President Harry Truman and his family move back into the completely rebuilt White House. Four years earlier, the piano of the president's daughter, Margaret, had proved too heavy for the floor. The reconstructed residence now has 132 rooms. You can visit the White House online at *http://www.whitehouse.gov/WH/kids/html/home.html*.

Investigate

How many average-size houses (don't count the bathrooms) could fit into the White House?

MARCH 28

1592

Johann Amos Comenius produces the first picture book for children.

Investigate

Look through a number of picture books and keep a tally of the number of pages in each.

Do you notice any patterns? Are there numbers that are consistent from book to book? Can you think of reasons why?

1903

Concert pianist Rudolf Serkin is born. He was considered to be an artist of unusual and impressive talents. He died on May 9, 1991. His son, Peter, is also a concern pianist.

Investigate

How long did Rudolf Serkin live?

A piano has 88 keys, some white and some black. Estimate the number of each and then count to check.

Poll how many of your classmates are learning to play the piano or any other musical instrument. Graph the results.

MARCH 29

1790

John Tyler, tenth U.S. president, is born. Tyler later fathers 15 children.

Investigate

What is the average number of children in your classmates' families?

Diagram Tyler's family tree to see how his descendents might multiply. If each descendant has two children, how many generations will it take to reach 1,000?

1886

Dr. John Pemberton introduces Coca-Cola at the soda fountain in his pharmacy. He describes it as a "brain tonic." Today, it is the world's most popular soft drink. In 1990 people in 155 countries drink 393 million Cokes every day. By 1993, they are drinking 705 million Cokes a day.

Investigate

Find out the per capita soft drink consumption of your classmates' families.

The record soda-can pyramid is built by five adults and five children at Dunhurst School in Petersfield, England, in 1994. They build a 4,900-can pyramid in 25 minutes 54 seconds. At a five-cents-a-can deposit, how much is the pyramid worth?

MARCH 30

1858

Hyman Lipman, of Philadelphia, receives a patent for a pencil with an attached eraser.

Investigate
In teams, set up an experiment that will answer the question: Can a pencil write more words or erase more words?

1923

Four hundred and forty passengers aboard the Cunard liner *Laconia* complete the first cruise to have circled the globe; 130 days have passed since they started.

Investigate
On what day did the cruise start?

MARCH 31

1889

The Eiffel Tower is completed. It was designed by Alexandre Gustave Eiffel for the Paris Exhibition. It is 984 feet tall and has 1,792 steps. You can check out the Eiffel

984'

1889 PARIS

The Eiffel Tower is completed.

Tower online at *http://metalab.unc.edu/louvre* or *http://www.louvre.fr*.

Investigate
About how long would it take you to climb the Eiffel Tower?

1998

St. Louis Cardinal Mark McGwire starts the baseball season by hitting a grandslam homerun. In his final at-bat this season (the 155th game he plays in, his 509th time at bat), he hits his 70th home run.

Investigate
On average, how many at-bats did McGwire have for each homerun? If you were pitching to him, would knowing when he'd had his last homer affect what you threw?

APRIL

April is Mathematics Education Month. For a free *Family Math Activities* brochure, send a business-size self-addressed stamped envelope to National Council of Teachers of Mathematics, 1906 Association Drive, Reston, VA 22091-1502.

APRIL 1

1960

TIROS 1 (TIROS stands for Television and Infra-Red Observation Satellite), the first of nine meteorological spacecraft, is launched. The spacecraft in this series provide wide- and narrow-angle television images and infrared data from which large-scale weather surveys are made. TIROS 1 is an 18-sided prism covered with 9,000 silicon solar cells

producing 28 volts of DC current. Over a 78-day period, TIROS 1 returns 22,952 images. Sixty percent of the pictures are of a quality good enough for meteorological research.

Investigate

Find out about how many pictures sent back from TIROS 1 are used for research.

1997

Hale-Bopp, the comet discovered independently in 1995 by Alan Hale and Thomas Bopp, the most distant comet ever discovered by amateurs, is at its brightest on this day, when it is closest to the Sun. The comet's official designation is C/1995 01. NASA observatories estimate that this comet has a monstrous nucleus of between

19 and 25 miles in diameter. The average comet nucleus is 3 miles in diameter or smaller. Hale-Bopp faded from view in the Northern Hemisphere in the late fall 1997. It will not appear again until 4397.

Investigate
How many years before Hale-Bopp returns?

APRIL 2

1902

The first motion picture theater opens in Los Angeles. The Electric Theater charged a dime to see an hour's entertainment, including the films *The Capture of the Biddle Brothers* and *New York in a Blizzard*.

Investigate
Mental Math: What does it cost today to see a movie in a theater? What percentage increase is the cost of admission over the 1902 cost?

1996

People in Christchurch, New Zealand, make a chocolate chip cookie with a diameter of $81\frac{2}{3}$ feet and an area of $5,241\frac{1}{2}$ square feet. It contains nearly 3 tons of chocolate.

Investigate
Bring a cookie to class and trace it on graph paper. Measure its diameter and figure its area.

Look at the diameter and area of the cookies your classmates have brought in. Do you see any patterns?

APRIL 3

1783

Author Washington Irving is born. Irving is the creator of Rip Van Winkle, the famous literary character who goes to sleep for twenty years.

1996 in New Zealand

Chocolate chip cookie

Investigate

How many hours do you sleep in a week? Figure out how many days all the hours you've slept in the last five years equal.

1866

Rudolph Eickemeyer and G. Osterheld patent the hat-shaping machine.

Investigate

Take a poll: What are the three most popular types of hat worn by your classmates? If you wear all three types of hat at once, one on top of the other, how many different ways can they be layered? What will happen if you add a fourth hat? Do you see a pattern?

APRIL 4

1818

The first United States flag is approved. Congress orders that the flag will always have 13 stripes, no matter how many states are added to the Union.

Investigate

Suppose Puerto Rico or Guam or both are added to the Union. Design a 51-state flag and a 52-state flag. Which is easier? Explain why.

1987

New York architect David R. Stein receives a patent for Bubble Thing, a device that enables the user to make bubbles eight feet in diameter. You can get some online advice about making bubbles at *http://bubbles.org*.

Investigate

Hold a class bubble contest. First put one quart of water in a two-quart bottle with a lid. Pour in four ounces of dishwashing detergent. Add three tablespoons of glycerin. Shake the mixture. Now invent "hoops" through which to blow bubbles. How will you measure who makes the biggest bubble?

APRIL 5

1621

The *Mayflower* sets sail from Plymouth, Massachusetts, returning to England and leaving the Plymouth colonists on their own. You can visit the *Mayflower* online at *http://members.aol.com/calebj/mayflower.html*.

Investigate

Mental Math: How many years ago did these colonists arrive in Plymouth?

1980

The world's most valuable stamp, an 1856 British Guiana one-cent magenta, is sold at auction for $850,000.

Investigate

Collect postmarks and stamps mailed from as many states as you can. Post them on a large outline map of the United States.

APRIL 6

1896

The first modern Olympic games open in Athens, Greece. The colors of the Olympic rings are blue, yellow, black, green, and red.

Investigate

Mental Math: How old are the modern Olympic games?

In how many sequences can three of the Olympic rings be arranged? If you find a pattern, use it to figure out the number of sequences in which all five rings can be arranged.

1930

James Dewar invents Twinkies, which become a famous junk food.

Investigate

Check out the package label on your favorite junk food. How much sodium and fat does a single serving contain? How many servings could you eat without going over the maximum amount of sodium and fat a person should eat in a day?

1864

The first camel race in America is held in Sacramento, California.

Investigate

Over distances of up to 6 miles (10 kilometers), a camel can run at an average speed of around 58 miles per hour (35 kilometers per hour). How does this compare with the running speed of horses? Dogs? Other animals?

1927

At Bell Laboratories in New York City, American Telephone and Telegraph president Walter Gifford hosts the first public demonstration of television broadcast from a distance. An image of Secretary of Commerce Herbert Hoover is transmitted to the audience in New York from Washington D.C.

Investigate

Keep a television diary for two weeks of when, what, and how long you watch. Make a graph of your results, and then combine your data with those of your classmates to create a class TV-watching graph.

1973

Pablo Picasso dies at age 91. Always experimenting, Picasso was influential in changing the course of modern art. He is particularly known for his experiments in Cubism, neo-Classicism, and Surrealism. He is also famous for his enormous output, producing about 140,000 paintings and drawings and 100,000 engravings.

For an extensive biography and sampling of Picasso's work, see *http://www.tamu.edu/mocl/picasso*.

Investigate

About how many pieces of art did Picasso create in a year, assuming he starts producing them at age 19 when he leaves Barcelona for Paris and paints about the same number each year? How many paintings do you do in a year?

1982

Steve Bentley makes it into the *Guinness Book of Records* by catching a Frisbee $272\frac{1}{2}$ feet from where he throws it. In 1995, Scott Stokely throws a Frisbee 656 feet, 2 inches. The distance record for women is 447 feet, 3 inches.

Investigate

Hold a Frisbee distance competition. Find a way to be sure your measurements are accurate.

1833

The first tax-supported free public library in the United States is founded, in Peterborough, New Hampshire.

Investigate

What percentage of the students in your class have a library card at the public library?

1853

Leaving Monroe County, Iowa, Amelia Stewart Knight, her husband, and their seven children start out for the Oregon Territory. Amelia notes in her diary that they travel eight miles the first day.

Investigate

At this rate, how long will it take this family to travel from Iowa to Oregon?

APRIL 10

1872

Nebraska holds the first Arbor Day. Since then, Nebraskans have planted ten million trees to commemorate this day, which is now celebrated nationally. Conservationists estimate that about 75,000 trees could be saved just by recycling the complete edition of a Sunday *New York Times*.

Investigate

Calculate the number of pages the local paper publishes each week. How many pounds would this be in one year?

Find out about local recycling policies and take charge of recycling your family's newspapers. If everyone in the U.S. recycled their newspapers, we would save 500,000 trees every week!

1982

Sir Ranulph Fiennes, Charles Burton, and Bothie the dog, of Great Britain, reach the North Pole, becoming the first team to cross both the North and South Poles in a single journey around the world.

An interview with Fiennes is available at *http://www.adventure-mag.com*. Search in "past expeditions."

Investigate

How far apart are the North and South Poles?

APRIL 11

1983

A twin-humped Bactrian camel is born at the St. Louis Zoo. The newborn weighs 80 pounds.

A Bactrian camel breeder in Spokane, Washington, has a Web site with pictures and data: *http://www.awesomewebmaster.com /bumpnmaya.htm*. The Lincoln Park Zoo also has camel data: *http://www.lpzoo.com*.

Investigate

How much did you weigh when you were born? Make a graph of the birthweights of your classmates.

How many average-weight human newborns would it take to equal the weight of this newborn camel?

1986

Dodge Morgan completes a record-breaking solo, nonstop, around-the-world trip in his six-foot boat American Promise. The 27,000-mile trip has taken him 150 days.

On April 11, 2000, runners compete in the Mt. Everest Marathon, starting at an altitude of 17,000 feet. The record time is 3 hours and 59 minutes. See *http://www .mountainzone.com*.

Investigate

When did Morgan begin his journey?

How many miles did he cover each day, on average?

APRIL 12

1803

James Monroe arrives in Paris intent on buying the city of New Orleans. He ends up making a deal to buy the whole Louisiana Territory, paying 15 million dollars for half a billion acres.

1934
New Hampshire

Investigate

How much did the United States pay per acre for this land?

Consult an atlas and determine the acreage of the state in which you live. What about your town: how many acres does it include?

1934

When Salvatore Pagliuca, meteorologist at the weather observatory on top of Mount Washington, in New Hampshire, takes the afternoon wind speed reading, he first ties a rope around his waist and asks two colleagues to hold the other end. They have a hard time preventing him from becoming a human kite. The wind speed is 231 miles an hour, the highest wind velocity ever directly recorded. The highest winds indirectly measured in the Earth's atmosphere, 287 miles per hour, were recorded in a tornado using Doppler radar. Mount Washington is famous for having periods of the worst weather in the world. It receives 246 inches of snow a year, and, on average, winds there are of hurricane force, over 75 miles per hour.

A great weather resource on the Internet can be accessed at *http://cirrus.sprl.umich.edu*. Extensive weather data about Mount Washington is available online at *http://www.mountwashington.org*.

Study weather charts for one week and then explain how mathematics is important to meteorologists.

Research the annual snowfall and maximum winds in your area. How do they compare with the Mount Washington data?

APRIL 13

1916

Funk Brothers Seed Company, of Bloomington, Iowa, sells the first shipment of hybrid seed corn to Samuel Ramsay, in Jacobsburg, Ohio, for 15 dollars a bushel. Hybrid seeds help farmers grow more corn per acre. In 1933, farmers used approximately one percent hybrid seed and get about 23 bushels of corn per acre. Today, farmers use over 96 percent hybrid seed and get 125 bushels per acre.

The National Corn Growers Association has a corn curriculum online at *http://www .ncga.com*.

Investigate
Use an almanac or similar resource to find out how many acres of corn are planted in the Corn Belt. How many bushels of corn will that many acres produce at 125 bushels per acre?

Americans eat about 500 million pounds of popcorn each year. There are about 250 million people in the U.S. How much popcorn is each person, on average, eating?

1966

Pan American World Airways places an order for the first 25 of the world's largest airplane, Boeing's 747. It can seat 490 passengers. The cabin of the plane is nearly 20 feet wide, allowing as many as 10 seats in each row.

Investigate
You've just been hired to design the seating plan for an airplane cabin holding 252 passengers. The first-class section needs to accommodate 12 passengers. Make a drawing to show your design.

APRIL 14

1970

Apollo 13 astronauts travel 248,655 miles from Earth, farther than anyone has yet gone. Their mission is to land on the moon, not go around it, but an explosion in an oxygen tank puts their spaceship off course. In their efforts to get safely back to Earth, they chart a course that takes them in a giant loop behind the moon. Their trip lasts almost six days.

The movie *Apollo* 13, based on this real-life drama, gives an exciting look at human ingenuity and problem solving, as well as the importance of mathematics. You can also log on to *http://spaceflight.nasa.gov* or *http://www.ksc.nasa.gov/history/apollo/apollo-*13 and get a behind-the-scenes look at the people who launch and fly space shuttles.

Investigate
The speed limit of many of our highways is 55 miles per hour. How long would it take to drive 248,655 miles at that speed? How does that compare to the almost six days Apollo 13 traveled?

1986

Hailstones weighing up to $2\frac{1}{2}$ pounds hit Bangladesh. Ninety-two people are killed.

Investigate
Estimate how much water it will take to make a block of ice that weighs $2\frac{1}{2}$ pounds. Then put that much water in a container and freeze it. Weigh the block of ice that results.

Was your estimate over or under? By how much?

APRIL 15

1912

The "unsinkable" luxury liner, *Titanic*, sinks at 2:27 A.M. The largest passenger vessel in the world goes under off the coast of Newfoundland about two and a half hours after striking an iceberg. In the end, 1,513 out of the 2,220 passengers perish in the freezing ocean water.

Investigate
Mental Math: How long ago did the Titanic sink?

Mental Math: How many survivors were there?

1997

A male boa constrictor named Popeye dies at the Philadelphia Zoo at the age of 40 years, 3 months, 14 days. This is the oldest a snake has been known to live.

Zoos report they can no longer accept donations of boas from people who want to give up their pets. You can take a virtual tour of the Philadelphia Zoo: *http://www.phillyzoo.org*.

Investigate
Figure your own age in years, months, days, and hours.

What was Popeye's date of birth?

APRIL 16

1900

The first books of postage stamps are issued: twelve 2-cent stamps cost 25 cents; twenty-four 2-cent stamps cost 49 cents; forty-eight 2-cent stamps cost 97 cents.

Investigate
Which book of stamps is the best buy?

How much would books of 12, 24, and 48 stamps cost at today's first-class rate?

1926

The Book-of-the-Month Club is founded.

Investigate
How many books would you have on the shelf if someone had given you a book every month you've been alive?

APRIL 17

1895

The first Hershey bar is sold. Poverty forced Milton Hershey to leave school in the fourth grade and take a job as an apprentice in a candy business. He grew up to build the largest chocolate factory in the world, in Hershey, Pennsylvania. In 1905 it had two million square feet of floor space.

Investigate
Bring a chocolate bar wrapper to class and the price of the chocolate. Make a list of all the different kinds of chocolate bars students bought, and note the weight and price of each. Which is the best buy per ounce?

1911

Eleven thousand seven hundred and forty-five immigrants arrive at Ellis Island, a record. Today, the population of every part of the United States except the South is at least 25 percent foreign-born.

Investigate
What percent of the students in your class were born in another country? Who comes from farthest away? What percent of your classmates' parents are foreign-born?

APRIL 18

1775

This evening Paul Revere starts out on his famous ride between Boston and Concord, Massachusetts—a distance of 12 miles and 390 yards—to warn, "The British are coming." In 1986, Ashrita Furman, of Queens, New York, somersaults the entire route in a little over ten hours; she takes 8,341 somersaults.

Investigate
How much distance does Furman cover in a single somersault?

1923

More than 74,000 fans show up for the opening day of the Yankees' new stadium in the Bronx. The stadium capacity was 58,000, but 74,200 fans crowd in.

For a brief history and lots of statistics about the stadium, see *http://www.ballparks.com* or *yankees.com*.

Investigate
Mental Math: How old is Yankee Stadium?

Can you figure out why the seating capacity for Yankee Stadium is smaller than when it was built?

How does the size of this crowd compare with the population of your school? of the town or city in which you live?

APRIL 19

1883

Richard von Mises, the Austrian mathematician noted for his work in statistics and probability, is born. In 1913 he teaches the first university course explaining powered flight. In 1915, he builds his own 600-horsepower airplane, thereby proving he knows what makes a plane stay up!

The site *http://www.teleport.com/~tcollins /monopoly.shtml* charts the long-term probabilities in playing Monopoly.

Investigate
Experiments can help you learn about probability. If you roll two dice and add the numbers that come up, you can get the sums of 2, 3, 4, 5, 6, and so on, up to 12. If you did this many times, what sums do you predict would come up more often? Less often? Have everyone in the class do ten trials. Collect and compile the data and analyze what happens.

1988

Two elephants arrive in Turin, Italy. They have walked 500 miles (805 kilometers) in 21 days, following the same route taken by Hannibal is his famous journey across the Alps from France.

Investigate
Mental Math: About how many miles do the elephants walk each day?

Time how long it takes you to walk half a mile. How many miles do you think you can walk in a day?

APRIL 20

1841

Naturalist, essayist, and individualist Henry David Thoreau, who takes pride in living off the land, notes in his journal, "To-day I earned seventy-five cents heaving manure out of a pen, and made a good bargain of it."

Investigate
How much does a person earn today in eight hours at the minimum wage?

If you did chores for a day, what do you think a fair wage would be? Which should pay more—heaving manure out of a pen,

1841

Henry David Thoreau

painting a fence, or answering a phone and taking messages?

1984

Twenty thousand people make a human chain around the U.S. Army Base in Mutlangen, Germany. They are protesting the nuclear missiles being kept in Western Germany.

Investigate
If all the students in your class join hands in a circle, what will the diameter of the circle measure? How many students would it take to circle the school? Use the information about your class circle to estimate.

APRIL 21

753 B.C.

Rome is founded. It becomes known as the eternal city.

Investigate
Mental Math: How old is Rome?

What interesting number fact can you see in the number 753?

When was the city you live in founded? Are there number facts to be discovered in this number?

1991

Moses Malone plays his 1,047th consecutive basketball game without fouling out. You can research foul-out statistics on other famous basketball players by logging on to the National Basketball Association's Web site: *http://www.nba.com.*

APRIL 22

1823

Roller skates are patented. In 1979, Theodore James Coombs skated from Los Angeles to New York City and as far back as Yates Center, Kansas—5,193 miles. Kimberly Ames holds the record for in-line speed skating. In 1994, she skated 283.07 miles in 24 hours.

Investigate
Mental Math: How long have roller skates been around?

About how long would it take Ames, skating at her record-setting speed and assuming she never has to rest, to do what Coombs did?

1878

The first Egg Roll is held on the grounds of the White House in Washington, D.C., attended by President Rutherford B. Hayes. The Egg Roll is still held the day after Easter on the South Lawn of the White House, hosted by the President of the United States and the First Lady. The Vice President and his wife also attend the event.

Investigate
Mental Math: For how many years has there been an Egg Roll at the White House?

How many Presidents have participated in the annual Egg Roll since it began?

APRIL 23

1564

William Shakespeare, poet and playwright, is born. In his lifetime, he writes thirty-seven plays and more than 150 sonnets. He dies on April 23, 1616.

Investigate
Mental Math: How long ago did William Shakespeare live?

1921

Charles Paddock sets a record time in the 300-meter track event by posting a time of 33.2 seconds. There is a zoo named after Paddock in Atascadero, CA. The cheetah at the zoo is probably the only animal that can run faster than Paddock did.

Investigate
Research the running speed of a cheetah and compare it to Charles Paddock's running speed.

Research the current record time for the 300-meter track event. How does it compare to Charles Paddock's record?

APRIL 24

1800

Congress establishes the Library of Congress, appropriating $5,000 "for the purchase of such books as may be necessary for the use of both Houses of Congress." These funds bought 740 books and 3 maps, which were shipped from England in 11 trunks. Today it is the largest library in the world, containing nearly 119 million items. You can visit the Library of Congress online at *http://lcweb.loc.gov.*

Investigate
About how much did each item in this first purchase cost, on average?

How could you estimate the number of volumes in the classroom library without counting every one?

APRIL 25

1901

New York is the first state to require license plates for cars. Plates cost $1.00. Today "vanity plates" are becoming increasingly popular with people who are willing to pay extra to have a license plate with their name or a special slogan.

Investigate
Using only six letters and/or numbers, create a license plate with a "message."

1959

The Saint Lawrence Seaway opens to traffic, saving shippers millions of dollars. By going from the sea to the Great Lakes across upstate New York, it is no longer necessary to ship goods over land.

Investigate
Construction of the Seaway began in January 1955. How long did it take to complete?

The cost was just over $470 million, of which Canada paid $336.5 million and the United States paid the rest. How much did the United States pay?

1993

Charles Servizio completes his 46,001st push-up in Fontana, California, 24 hours after he does his first one.

Investigate

How many push-ups does Servizio average each minute? How does that compare with your own efforts?

How many minutes does Servizio keep doing push-ups?

APRIL 26

1822

Frederic Law Olmsted, the future landscape architect who will design Central Park in New York City, is born.

Investigate

Discuss how math thinking and skills are necessary for architects.

Walk around outside on a mathematically related "living things" treasure hunt. Sketch a living thing that is as wide as your hand span; as long as your foot; about the same height as you are; that reaches your knees; and so on.

1900

Charles Richter is born. He later devises the Richter scale of earthquake measurement, a scale that measures the ground motion and determines the amount of energy released at the epicenter. On Richter's scale, each number indicates a tenfold increase in seismic wave activity; in other words, a level 4 earthquake is ten times greater than a level 3. Online information about earthquakes can be found at *http://www.civeng.carleton .ca/cgi-bin/quakes*.

Investigate

If a level 5 earthquake is 100 times greater than a level 3, how much greater is a level 6 than a level 3?

APRIL 27

1898

Ludwig Bemelmans, author of the six beloved *Madeline* books, is born. The first book is published in 1939. In these books, twelve little girls live in an old house in Paris; when they go out, they always line up in two straight lines.

Investigate
Mental Math: How old was Ludwig Bemelmans when the first *Madeline* book was published?

What other ways could the little girls line up so that there were always the same number in each line?

1937

The first social security account numbers are issued. The Social Security Act was approved by President Franklin Delano Roosevelt in 1935 with the intent of offering assistance to the aged, the blind, and dependent children who have lost a parent.

Investigate
What percentage of a person's paycheck goes to social security today? If a person's monthly paycheck is $3000, how much will be deducted for social security?

Bring in the first five numbers from your social security number. Do you notice anything interesting about the numbers?

APRIL 28

1937

The first animated-cartoon electric sign is displayed on a building on Broadway in New York City. It contains 2000 lightbulbs.

Investigate
Do you think there are more or less than 2000 lightbulbs in your home? in your school? How could you make a reliable estimate?

1975

World Whale Day introduces the slogan and the sentiment "Save the Whales." Weighing approximately 140 tons and stretching more than 100 feet (30 meters), the blue whale is the largest mammal that has ever lived. It is hunted for its meat and oil and may now exist in numbers too low for survival. The humpback whale is also endangered. You can find out about whale-watching expeditions—and discover links to other whale-related Web sites—at *http://www.physics.helsinki.fi/whale*. Also, *http://www.whaletimes.org* has many whale facts. For example, blue whale calves can gain as much as 200 pounds (90 kilograms) a day.

Investigate
About how many fifth graders would it take to equal the weight of one blue whale?

1975 World Whale Day — SAVE THE WHALES!

APRIL 29

1913

Gideon Sundback receives a patent for a hookless fastening; it becomes knows as the zipper.

Investigate:
What percentage of your pants, skirts, or dresses contain zippers? How about jackets?

1995

The *Challenger* is launched from Kennedy Space Center, Florida, with a crew of seven and an animal menagerie including monkeys and rats. It lands at Edwards Air Force Base, California, on May 6, after 111 orbits of the Earth.

Investigate
What was the approximate duration of a single orbit?

APRIL 30

1891

The National Zoological Park (*http://www.si.edu/natzoo*) opens in Washington, D.C. It is situated on 175 acres and has been designed by landscape architect Frederick Law Olmsted. So many people, including Alexander Graham Bell and Theodore Roosevelt, give animals to the zoo that it has to turn down an offer of 18 bison from Buffalo Bill Cody.

Investigate
Take a poll: What are the top five favorite animals your classmates want to see at the zoo? Collect information and organize it into a class graph.

The difficulties of zoos accepting gift animals can be understood when you realize a bison needs at least three acres of grassland. How many acres would 18 bison need?

1952

Mr. Potato Head becomes the first toy to be advertised on TV. According to a Potato Head time line on *http://www.mrpotatohead.com*, in 1953 Mr. Potato Head married Mrs. Potato Head and in 1985 Baby Potato Head was born. In 1995, Mr. Potato Head appeared in the movie *Toy Story*.

Investigate
Mental Math: How old was Mr. Potato Head when he appeared in *Toy Story*?

Count how many toys are advertised on TV during a half-hour Saturday-morning show aimed at kids. Compare statistics and figure out the typical number of Saturday-morning advertisements you could see in a year.

1942

MAY

1873

The first U.S. postcard, measuring 3 inches by $5\frac{1}{8}$ inches, is issued. It is imprinted with a one-cent stamp bearing the likeness of the Goddess of Liberty.

Dear Saunis,
I'm having a good time.
Hawaii is beautiful. I'll
be home soon.
X XOO
Ted

S. Parsons
Kent
Ohio

1873

Investigate

Along with each of your classmates, bring to class a stamped postcard addressed to the person your family knows who lives the farthest distance away in the United States. Write a message on the card, mail it, and stick a pin on the wall map marking the card's destination. Now figure out how many miles your card has to travel. As a class, figure the total miles all of your cards will travel.

1926

The 267-foot-tall "General Grant" tree, in General Grant National Park, California, is officially designated the nation's Christmas tree. The diameter of the "General Grant" at the base is 40.3 feet; at 200 feet above the ground, its diameter is about 12 feet. The tree is between 3,500 and 4,000 years old.

More information and pictures are available at *http://www.nps.gov/seki/grantpic.htm.*

Investigate
Do you think all the students in your class will fit inside a circle with a 40.3-foot diameter? On the playground, draw a circle with diameter of 40.3 feet and then see how many children can stand inside that circle.

MAY 2
1803

France sells the Louisiana Territory, 828,000 square miles, to the United States for 80 million francs, or 15 million U.S. dollars.

You can read the purchase agreement online at *http://www.nara.gov/exhall/originals /louistxt.html.*

Investigate
Figure out how much one franc was worth in U.S. money. Look at a money conversion table and see what a franc is worth in U.S. money today.

1969

The *Queen Elizabeth* 2 (or QE2) sets sail on her maiden voyage. The ship carries 1,400 passengers from South Hampton, England, to New York City. It takes 4 days, 16 hours, 35 minutes. Lots of statistics and photos of the QE2 are available at *http://www.qe2.org.uk.*

Investigate
The QE2 has a crew of 1015 people and carries 1810 passengers. How does this ratio compare with the number of students attending your school and the number of

staff working there? Can you explain the differing needs on a cruise ship and in a school?

MAY 3
1849

Jacob Riis, Danish-American photographer, is born. As a police reporter in New York City, Riis becomes familiar with the desperate conditions in slum areas. Documenting the conditions through his photographs and articles, Riis leads a movement for the establishment of playgrounds and improved water supplies in slum areas.

Investigate
How does the total time you spend in school compare with time you spend playing at recess or lunchtime?

How does the area of your school playground compare with the total area of school classrooms?

1904

The first speed limits in the United States are decreed by New York State. They are 10 miles per hour in cities and 20 miles per hour in the country.

Investigate
Plan a 1,000-mile trip, and then figure out how long it would take to complete it at the 1904 speed limits.

MAY 4
1626

Peter Minuit, first Director General of New Amsterdam, arrives at the Dutch colony at the mouth of the Hudson River. Later he buys the island of "manhattes" from the Native Americans for goods worth about 60 guilders, or $24.

Investigate
Make a list of a total of five things you could buy that cost about $24 all together. How many dollars are 60 Dutch guilders worth today?

1845

The first iron truss bridge with parallel chords is completed, in Pottstown, Pennsylvania, on the main line of the Philadelphia and Reading Railroad Company. It has a 34.2-foot span and remains in place until 1901.

Truss bridges use strong, rigid frameworks by fastening beams together in a triangular configuration. The truss framework distributes the load of the bridge in a way that allows a relatively lightweight bridge to carry heavy loads.

The Bridges Project is an extensive resource of bridge data: *http://www.civil.rice.edu /bridgesproject*.

Investigate
Architecture students build truss bridges with toothpicks—and learn something important about the strength of this design. Check out books in the library for information on building model bridges.

MAY 5

1961

Alan Shepard becomes the first American in space. He makes a 15-minute-22-second suborbital flight in the Mercury spacecraft *Freedom 7*. Shepard enters the spacecraft at 5:15 A.M. Eastern Standard Time. Liftoff occurs at 9:34 A.M. *Freedom 7* reaches an altitude of 116 miles (187 kilometers). It splashes down in the Atlantic 302 miles from Cape Canaveral 15 minutes, 22 seconds after launch. The NASA Web site is *http://spaceflight.nasa.gov/shuttle/index.html*.

Investigate
What time is it when the spacecraft splashes down?

1989

The spacecraft *Magellan* begins an 800-million-mile journey to Venus. You can take a look at Venus online at *http://pds.jpl.nasa.gov /planets*.

Investigate
How many trips from New York to San Francisco and back again would equal one million miles? How many trips from your home to school and back?

MAY 6

1954

British medical student Roger Bannister becomes the first person to run a mile in less than four minutes. He does it in 3 minutes, 59.4 seconds.

Investigate
Create a graph depicting the record running times for the mile from Bannister's time to the present.

1994

Queen Elizabeth II of Britain and President François Mitterrand of France dedicate the English Channel Tunnel, popularly known as "the Chunnel." The Chunnel, running under water 23.6 miles between Folkestone, England, and Calais, France, cost more that 15 billion dollars and took six years to build. Commercial traffic begins on November 14.

A geography unit detailing trade and environmental concerns to the Chunnel is available at *http://www.mcrel.org/resources /plus/chunnel.asp*.

At full speed, the train travels at one kilometer in twelve seconds. How fast does it go in kilometers per hour? Can you translate this speed into miles per hour?

MAY 7

1983

Students from Carroll High School, Yakima, Washington, wash 3,844 cars in eight hours.

Investigate

About how many cars did the students wash each hour? How many students do you think participated in washing cars? Explain your reasoning.

1988

Randall Schneider skips rope for 22 hours, 5 minutes, 2 seconds at the Wisconsin State Fair.

Investigate

Devise a plan for figuring out how many "skips" Schneider's marathon represents.

MAY 8

1884

Harry Truman is born. Although he became president on April 12, 1945, Harry Truman did not sleep in the White House until May 7, after giving the recently widowed Eleanor Roosevelt time to remove her belongings. The next morning, his birthday, he writes to his mother and sister: "I am sixty-one this morning, and I slept in the President's room in the White House last night."

You can visit the Truman Library online—it has a special kids' section: *http://www.trumanlibrary.org*.

Investigate

Figure out how many nights have passed since you were born.

1924

Tana Hoban, future photographer and author, is born. Hoban's photographs call attention to the shape, size, and color of everyday objects and to relationships between these objects.

Investigate

See how many geometric shapes you can spot in your classroom.

MAY 9

1873

British archaeologist and Egyptologist Howard Carter is born in London. In 1922, he makes one of the greatest archaeological finds of the 20th century. In the valley of the tombs of the Kings in Luxor, Egypt, he and the Earl of Carnarvon discover the tomb of Tutankhamen, a pharaoh who reigned in the 14th century B.C. In the burial chamber, they find four gilded shrines nestled one inside the other. The outermost shrine measures 17 feet by 11 feet and 9 feet high. The innermost of these covered a stone sarcophagus. Inside that were three coffins—the innermost being made of 110 kg. of solid gold. Inside lay the pharaoh himself, wearing the famous gold mask.

There are numerous Egyptology sites on the Web. Here are a few: *http://www.nationalgeographic.com/egypt*; *http://www.pbs.org/wgbh/nova/pyramid*; *http://www.kv5.com/intro/html*; and *http://www.metmuseum.org*.

Investigate

Estimate if your classroom is bigger or smaller than the outermost burial shrine. Measure the length of two students lying head to foot on the floor, and then estimate again. Estimate and then measure the classroom.

1984

A 24-foot-high mobile, *Big Crinkly*, by Alexander Calder, sells at auction for $852,000.

Investigate
Discover the principles of mobiles by making one.

MAY 10

1869

The Union Pacific and Central Pacific railways meet at Promontory Point, Utah. The governor of California drives the last spike, a gold one, completing the tracks of the first transcontinental railroad. The Union Pacific Railroad had begun construction at Omaha, Nebraska, and the Central Pacific, at Sacramento, California.

Investigate
Consult a map and figure out the length of this railroad.

1996

Bryan Berg, of Spirit Lake, Iowa, completes a 100-story house made of playing cards. It reaches a height of 19 feet, 2 inches.

Investigate
Estimate a distance of 19 feet and then measure to see how accurate your estimate is.

MAY 11

1967

Ceremonies mark the installation of the 100 millionth telephone in the United States. In the 1990s people in the United States made more than 421 billion phone calls a year.

Investigate
Keep track of how many times your family's phone rings on a Thursday night and on a Saturday night. What's the proportion of calls received on Thursday to those received on Saturday?

1990

Australian Timothy John Macartney-Snape ends his 745-mile trek to the peak of Mt. Everest, becoming the first person to ascend the entire altitude—from sea level at the Bay of Bengal to the summit—on foot.

In May 2000, Babu Chhiri, a Sherpa guide, makes the trek in less than sixteen hours—from the base camp to the summit.

There is lots of Everest lore online at *http://www.mnteverest.net*. Here's the Everest site of a third-grade class: *http://www.newton.mec.edu/angier/ferguson/everest/home.html*.

Investigate
Research some mathematical facts related to Mt. Everest.

MAY 12

1777

Philip Lenzi, a confectioner from New York, displays the first public advertisement for ice cream. Records show that during the summer of 1790 George Washington ran up an ice cream bill of about $200, roughly equivalent to $6,000 in today's money.

Investigate
If you have three flavors of ice cream, how many different two-flavor ice cream cones can you make? What if you have four flavors?

If a two-dip ice cream cone costs $1.50, how many can you buy for $6,000?

1777 — New York

1985

In Sacramento, California, a truck carrying hives overturns and 4,000,000 bees swarm over the freeway.

Investigate
How do you think the truck driver knew how many bees the hives contained? (Hint: There are about 60,000 bees in one hive.)

MAY 13

1942

A two-seater army helicopter takes off from Stratford, Connecticut. Four days later, after flying at low altitudes and making sixteen stops en route, it eventually ends its journey at Wright Field, in Dayton, Ohio, 761 miles away. Actual flying time is 16 hours, 10 minutes.

Investigate
Make a rough estimate of how fast this helicopter was flying.

How long would it take a helicopter to make that trip these days?

MAY 14

1634

Governor William Bradford signs the first property tax law in the Massachusetts colony. This law says that people should pay taxes according to the wealth of their estate, not according to how large their families are.

Investigate
Come up with a tax system you consider fair.

1804

At the request of President Thomas Jefferson, a military and scientific expedition led by Captain Meriwether Lewis (Jefferson's private secretary) and William Clark leaves St. Louis to explore the Louisiana Purchase. Their three boats carry 21 bales of gifts for Native Americans, 50 kegs of pork, 3,400 pounds of flour, and 750 pounds of salt, among other items. The expedition returned 832 days later.

Investigate
Locate a biscuit recipe and figure out how many biscuits 3,400 pounds of flour will make.

MAY 15

1903

President Theodore Roosevelt meets celebrated naturalist and author John Muir in California, and they take a trip through Yosemite together. Roosevelt later recalls, "Lying out at night under those giant sequoias was like lying in a temple built by no hand of man, a temple grander than any human architect could by any possibility build, and I hope for the preservation of

May 15, 1903 — Yosemite, California

the groves of giant trees simply because it would be a shame to our civilization to let them disappear."

Giant sequoias are the most massive trees in the world. Most of their mass is found at the bottom. The "General Sherman," for example, is 274.9 feet tall, has a ground-level circumference of 78.7 feet, and weighs about 3,150 tons.

You can visit Yosemite online at *http:parks.yahoo.com/parks/parks/yose*.

Investigate
Research the weight of three big things and compare those weights with that of the "General Sherman" sequoia.

How might you use math to decide if a visit in peak tourist season—June through August—is better or worse than a visit in the low tourist season—February?

1942

Gasoline rationing to aid the World War II effort goes into effect. Each family is allowed three gallons a week.

Investigate
How far could your family drive using only three gallons of gas a week? Where could you go?

How many gallons of gas does your family use in a week? Make a class graph.

MAY 16

1866

Congress authorizes coinage of the nickel. It weighs 77.16 grains and is made up of 75 percent copper and 25 percent nickel. In 1938, a contest was held to design a new nickel; the Jefferson nickel was the result. Near the date on a nickel is a mark identifying where the nickel was minted.

In 1999, 1,212,000,000 nickels were minted in Philadelphia; 1,066,720,000 were minted in Denver.

You can find out about coins online at *http://www.usmint.gov*.

Investigate
Examine four nickels. Where was each one minted? How many miles away from where you live are these mints located?

1975

Japanese mountaineer Junko Tabei is the first woman to climb the 29,028-foot (8,848-meter) peak of Mt. Everest.

Investigate
Calculate how many round-trips between home and school you'd have to make to equal the distance Junko Tabei climbed.

MAY 17

1845

The rubber band is patented.

Investigate

Along with your classmates, assemble a collection of rubber bands of various lengths and thicknesses. Then research their stretchability. Record each band's unstretched length (lay it alongside a ruler to find out). Then hang weights on the band until it will not stretch further and measure this new length.

1973

Matthew McGrory is born in Pennsylvania. He grows up to wear size-23 shoes. Anthropologists Paul Aabell and Dr. Mary Leakey have discovered footprints in Tanzania, dating back 3.6 million years, that were made by a person who was about 3 feet, 11 inches tall. The largest dinosaur footprints were found in 1932, in Salt Lake City; the prints measure $53\frac{1}{2}$ inches long and 32 inches wide.

Investigate

Trace one of your feet on construction paper and cut it out. How many of your feet tall are you? Put the cut-out feet in order according to students' heights, with the foot of the shortest student first, up to the foot of the tallest student. What do you notice about the lengths of the feet?

Measure the length and width of your feet; how does this proportion relate to the proportion of the dinosaur prints?

MAY 18

1852

Massachusetts passes a law stating that children "between the ages of eight and fourteen years" must attend school for twelve weeks in the year.

Investigate

How many hours do you attend school each year? What fraction of every day are you at school?

1986

A bullfrog named Rosie the Ribeter sets a record at the annual Calaveras County Jumping Frog Jubilee in Angels Camp, California, by jumping a total of 21 feet, $5\frac{3}{4}$ inches in three consecutive leaps. The record still stands in 2000.

Investigate

Estimate how far you think you can jump. Then make a series of three standing broad jumps and carefully measure each one. How do you compare with Rosie?

MAY 19

1844

Ralph Waldo Emerson sends some pencils made by his friend Henry David Thoreau to another friend. The pencils cost 75 cents a dozen. Today people who work at the New York Stock Exchange use about one million pencils a year.

1973

SIZE 23

Estimate how many pencils you and your classmates will use this year.

Set up an experiment to determine how long a pencil lasts.

1857

William Francis Channing, of Boston, Massachusetts, and Moses Gerrish Farmer, of Salem, Massachusetts, receive a patent for the first electric fire alarm system. Boston had already voted to test this system in June 1851.

Investigate
On a floor plan of your house, indicate the fire escape route from your bedroom. Include the number of feet you have to travel.

MAY 20
1875

The International Bureau of Weights and Measures is established. (At one point in history, a king's foot was considered the standard of measure.) The intricacies of the two standard systems of weights and measures can be found online at *http://lamar.colostate.edu/~hillger/everyday.htm*.

Investigate
Measure the feet of a number of adults you know. Compile the results. Why is the length of a particular person's foot not a good standard of measure?

1978

Fifty-three-year-old Mavis Hutchinson becomes the first woman to run across America. She averaged 45 miles a day, and it has taken her 69 days.

Investigate
About how many miles did Mavis Hutchinson run?

MAY 21
1874

Nellie Grant, daughter of President Ulysses S. Grant, marries Algernon Sartoris in the East Room in the White House. Wedding guests are served a wedding breakfast consisting of cream of celery soup, grilled trout, mushrooms in cream on toast, venison with plum sauce, potato chips, green peas served in pastry shells, fruit cup, quail with pureed chestnuts, tomato aspic with walnuts and celery, and pistachio ice cream with whipped cream.

It's a fact: Americans eat about 1,400 pounds of food per capita each year.

Investigate
How many pounds of food, per capita, do Americans eat every day? Take a poll to determine your class's favorite breakfast menu.

What would you serve if 100 guests were coming to breakfast? Do choices change according to the number of guests?

1977

Santjie, a South African sharp-nosed frog, achieves the greatest distance covered by a frog in a triple jump, 33 feet $5\frac{1}{2}$ inches, at a frog derby in South Africa.

Here's the frog page of a fifth-grade class: *http://www.esd113.wednet.edu/frogs*. A Thousand Friends of Frogs also has a Web site: *http://cgee.hamline.edu/frogs*.

Investigate
It isn't hard to measure how far a frog jumps, but how do you measure a frog? Write a letter to the frog keeper at the zoo giving him

or her some advice on frog measuring. You may include drawings.

MAY 22

1570

Abraham Ortelius publishes an atlas in Belgium. Atlases are the source of a great deal of fascinating information.

Investigate
Search an atlas for two number facts about your state that you think no one else will find. Create a math problem using these numbers.

1819

The *Savannah* leaves Savannah, Georgia, for Liverpool, England, and becomes the first steamship to cross the Atlantic. She makes the trip in 29 days, 11 hours. She is also a full-rigged sailing ship and sails under steam for about 85 hours of the trip. (The first crossing under steam power alone is made by the *Great Western*, in 1838; she makes the trip in 15 days.)

Investigate
What percentage of the time was the *Savannah* assisted by sails?

MAY 23

1895

The New York Public Library is incorporated. It now has 85 neighborhood libraries and four research libraries, with 16 million users who enter their doors each year.

Investigate
How many books do you estimate are in your school library? Find out.

How many books do you estimate are borrowed each year from your school library? Check with the librarian to find out.

1936

Peter Parnall, future children's author-illustrator, is born. Parnall is noted for his careful drawings of the natural world.

Investigate
Look at some of Parnall's artwork, and then go outside and make a "mathematically accurate" drawing of an object you discover.

MAY 24

1844

In Washington, D.C., Samuel F. B. Morse demonstrates that he can send instant messages from one city to another by telegraph. Morse sends his message 41 miles from the Capitol building to the Democratic National Convention, in Baltimore. Using the dot-and-dash code he invented, Morse's message was "What hath God wrought?" He was asking the convention who they had nominated as their presidential candidate.

There's a Morse code "translator" online. Users input a message and then see—and hear—it written in Morse code: *http://www.soton.ac.uk/~scp93ch/morse/start.html*. The Samuel F. B. Morse historic site is at *http://www.morsehistoricsite.org*.

Investigate
Invent your own code using numbers. Then try to "break" your classmates' codes.

1988

In Los Angeles, California, John Moschitta recites 545 words in 55.8 seconds, or 586 words per minute. Most people cannot speak comprehensibly above 300 words per minute. In 1992, a rapper made it into *The Guinness Book of World Records* by rapping 674 syllables in 54.9 seconds. The entry documenting this feat doesn't indicate whether anybody could understand what he said.

Investigate
Set up a speed-talking experiment. (Hint: Most speed talkers pick a set piece to read.)

MAY 25

1856

Mark Twain writes a letter in which he complains of being pestered by a chorus of "forty-seven thousand mosquitoes and twenty-three thousand horse flies."

There are mosquito facts online at *http://www.rci.rutgers.edu/~insects/moslife.htm*. Fun facts can be found at *http://www.education.wisc.edu/outreach/mosquitoes*.

Investigate
Make up a math problem using some of these mosquito facts:

◆ There are 2,700 species of mosquitoes.

◆ A mosquito weighs about 2 to 2.5 milligrams.

◆ A mosquito can smell a host 20 to 35 miles away.

◆ A mosquito can fly 1 to 1.5 miles per hour.

◆ A female mosquito drinks 5 millionths of a liter of blood per serving. (Only female mosquitoes bite.)

1935

Jesse Owens sets the world long-jump record with a jump of 26 feet, $8\frac{1}{4}$ inches. He also breaks two world sprint records and ties a third. The official Jesse Owens Web site is *http://www.cmgww.com/sports/owens*.

Investigate
How many students lying head to foot will it take to equal the distance of Owens's jump?

MAY 26

1826

Thomas Jefferson reveals his eye for penny-pinching when he notes in his journal that a gallon of lamp oil costing $1.25 has lit his room for six hours a night for twenty-five nights.

Investigate
Keep your own "lights on" log: for one week, check how many light bulbs are on every hour from when you get home from school to when you go to bed. Keep track of how many light bulbs you turn off. What conclusions do you reach about "lights on" in your home?

1969

The command module of *Apollo* 10, carrying Col. Thomas Patten Stafford, Cdr. Eugene Andrew Cernan, and Cdr. John Watts Young, reaches a speed of 24,791 miles per hour. This is the fastest speed at which humans have traveled.

Investigate
Identify some place on Earth you would like to visit, and then figure out how long it would take to get there traveling at this speed.

MAY 27

1767

Thomas Jefferson notes in his garden journal that he has planted lettuce, radish, broccoli, and cauliflower seeds.

Investigate
Keep a vegetable journal for one week: write down all the vegetables you eat. Then,

with your classmates, make a graph showing the most popular vegetables.

1931

Swiss physicist Auguste Piccard and his fellow scientist Paul Kipfer become the first men to reach the Earth's stratosphere. Taking off in a huge hydrogen-filled balloon from Augsburg, Germany, they rise to 50,135 feet (15,281 meters). They land safely on a glacier in the Austrian Tyrol. The purpose of their journey is to study the sun's cosmic rays.

For balloon model projects (adult supervised) made with dry cleaner bags and birthday candles, see *http://www.overflite.com*. Tables show how vital mathematics is to balloon flight.

Investigate

Estimate the number of miles this balloon ascends. Compare this height with the cruising altitude of today's jet passenger planes.

MAY 28

1892

The Sierra Club, a group dedicated to the preservation and expansion of the world's parks, wildlife, and wilderness areas, is founded by Scottish-American conservationist John Muir. Muir's work leads to the development of the U.S. National Park system.

Investigate

Mental Math: How old is the Sierra Club? Research important statistical data about the nearest national park.

1959

Able (a Rhesus monkey) and Baker (a squirrel monkey) are launched into space in the nose cone of a *Jupiter* missile. They reach an altitude of 300 miles and a distance of 1,500 miles while traveling at speeds of over 10,000 miles per hour. The purpose is to test spacecraft life support systems and the effects of space flight on primates. The nose cone lands in the Atlantic Ocean 1,500 miles (2,400 kilometers) from the launch pad at Cape Canaveral, Florida. The monkeys experienced 4.2 minutes of weightlessness. This mission is the first recovery of living beings after their return from space.

Animal astronaut facts are available online at *http://ham.spa.umn.edu/kris/animals .html*

nose cone: 9'
tank and shaft: 51'
launch stand: 7'3"
diameter of nosecone: 5'5"
diameter of tank and shaft: 8'4"
weight empty: 11,000 lbs.
weight fueled for launch: 198,000 lbs.

Investigate

What is the distance of the *Jupiter* missile from the tip of the nose cone to the ground?

MAY 29

1935

Hoover Dam is completed; it is a concrete plug of about seven million tons in a Colorado River canyon 1,244 feet wide and 726 high. It is built in concrete block or vertical columns varying in size from 60 feet square to about 25 feet square. Its maximum depth is 500 feet. Seventeen generators convert the waterpower into electricity, producing six billion kilowatt-hours of electricity a year. The hydroelectric power is used in Nevada, Arizona, and California.

The Hoover Dam's official Web site is

http://www.hooverdam.com. A transcript of the PBS program about the Hoover Dam and a teachers' guide are available from *http://www.pbs.org/wgbh/amex/hoover/index.htm.*

Investigate
Nevada uses 25 percent of the Hoover Dam's power, Arizona 19 percent. How much does California use? Why does it get the most?

1942

Bing Crosby records the song *White Christmas,* written by Irving Berlin. Forty million copies of this record have been sold, making it the biggest-selling single ever.

Stormfax lists the probability of a White Christmas for every area of the country—compiled by the National Climatic Data Center: *http://www.stormfax.com/whtexmas.htm.*

Investigate
It's December in May! Ask as many adults as you can what their favorite Christmas song is, and compile a class graph displaying the results.

1922

One hundred thousand people attend the dedication of the Lincoln Memorial, in Washington, D.C. Congress passed a law authorizing the monument in 1867, but Daniel Chester French was not chosen to sculpt the statue of Lincoln until 1914. French first made a 3-foot model; then he enlarged it to 7 feet. Finally he decided that the finished statue should be 19 feet high, measuring from Lincoln's foot to the top of his head; the chair Lincoln sits in measures $12\frac{1}{2}$ feet high from seat to floor. The statue was shipped in 28 pieces from New York City, where it was carved, and assembled at the memorial site.

Information about the memorial is online at: *http://www.nps.gov/linc/statue.htm.*

Investigate
In pairs, measure each other sitting down. What is the distance from the foot to the top of the head? Next, measure a child much younger than you sitting down, and an adult sitting down. Examine all these measurements. What conclusions can you make?

1971

Mariner 9 is launched. On November 13th, it becomes the first spacecraft to fly by Mars. Current Mars explorations are discussed online at *http://www.nasa.gov/nasa/nasa_hottopics.html* and *http://seds.lpl.arizona.edu/nineplanets/nineplanets/nineplanets.html.*

Investigate
How long does it take *Mariner* 9 to reach Mars? Guess how far away Mars is, and then look it up.

MAY 31

1907

Taxis arrived in New York City.

Investigate
Research the rates for taxis in your own or a neighboring town or city. How much would it cost you to take a taxi from your home to school?

1983

The Kansas City (Missouri) zoo sells footprints of an elephant named Lois to raise money to enlarge the elephant quarters.

The zoo is online at *http://www .kansascityzoo.org*.

Investigate
With a parent's permission, take an ink paw print of your (or a neighbor's) pet. What is the circumference of the paw? How wide is it? How long? How does this compare with the pet's overall height?

J U N E

JUNE 1

1925

Yankee first baseman Lou Gehrig begins his 14-year streak of playing in 2,130 games. This streak ends May 2, 1939. This phenomenal record earns Gehrig the nickname "Iron Horse." You can visit major league baseball online at *http://www.majorleaguebaseball.com.*

Investigate

Check box scores for a week. How many outs during a game typically involve the first baseman? Estimate how many outs Gehrig makes in 14 years.

1933

The Federal Barge Line steamer *Vicksburg,* towing barges carrying coffee, sisal, and general merchandise, leaves New Orleans, Louisiana. The towed barges are transferred to the H*oover* at Memphis, to the *Sawyer* for the trip up the Illinois River, and to the *Warner* at Ottaway, Illinois. The towed barges arrive in Chicago on June 21, completing the first trip on the Lakes-to-the-Gulf Waterway.

Investigate

Here's a logic puzzler: Three barges, one filled with coffee, one filled with sisal, and one filled with general merchandise, are headed for three different destinations— Chicago, Memphis, and New Orleans. Figure out which one is going where based on the following information:

1. The load of coffee is not going to New Orleans.
2. The load of sisal will end up where the coffee starts.
3. The coffee starts at the city that is farthest east of the three.

JUNE 2

1933

President Franklin D. Roosevelt officially accepts the first White House swimming pool, paid for by public donations. Located in the west terrace of the White House, it is 50 feet long and 15 feet wide; the depth ranges from 4 to 8 feet.

Investigate
Estimate how long a distance of 50 feet is. How many students lying end to end will it take to equal 50 feet? Is there anything in your school that is about 50 feet long?

1966

The first U.S. *Surveyor* satellite lands on the moon and begins sending back television pictures. Launched on May 30, it has traveled 231,483 miles in 63 hours, 36 minutes. You can check out lunar-related information at *http://shuttle.nasa.gov*, *http://pds.jpl.nasa.gov/planets*, and *http://seds.lpl.arizona.edu/nineplanets/nineplanets/nineplanets.html*.

Investigate
Use a calculator to figure out at what speed the *Surveyor* traveled.

JUNE 3

1899

The International Ladies Garment Workers Union is founded by cloakmakers in New York City.

Investigate
Along with your classmates, check the labels on the clothing you are wearing. Where was it made? What percentage/fraction of clothing being worn by the class is made outside the United States?

1981

Twelve tornadoes touch down in Denver, Colorado, a rare occurrence because tornadoes form when very humid air meets dry air. That's why Florida has, on average, more than twice as many tornadoes as Colorado—even though Colorado is almost twice as big. By and large, states in the Far West and the Northeast get few tornadoes. Texas averages more tornadoes a year than any other state: 124. The United States averages 1,000 tornadoes every year.

Investigate
Find out the number of tornadoes that occur in your state each year. What percentage of the U.S. total is this? Check *http://www.ncdc.noaa.gov/ol/climate/severeweather/tornadoes.html*.

JUNE 4

1896

Henry Ford's first car is assembled in Detroit, but the test drive is postponed when workmen discover the finished car is wider than the door of the shed in which it has been built. Later, when Ford starts mass-producing cars, he says people can have any color they want—as long as it is black . . . because black paint dries the fastest.

You can learn about the Model T online at *http://www.hfmgv.org*.

Investigate
How many cars do you think Ford Motor Company now manufactures in a year? Make an estimate and then write to the company to find out.

1896
Detroit, Michigan

Set up a car watch: what fraction of the total number of cars that drive by the school are black? white? other colors?

1912

Massachusetts passes the first minimum wage law.

Investigate
How much will a 15-cent increase in the minimum wage come to in a year's time, assuming a worker is paid for 52 thirty-five-hour weeks?

JUNE 5
1914

A two-year-old American alligator arrives at the Adelaide Zoo, in South Australia. She lives there until she dies at the age of 66, the longest an alligator is known to have lived. (You can tell an alligator from a crocodile by checking the lower fourth tooth: a crocodile's tooth protrudes when its mouth is closed; an alligator's doesn't.)

Alligators have about 80 teeth in their mouth at one time. When a tooth wears down, a new tooth replaces it. An alligator can go through 2,000 to 3,000 teeth in a lifetime.

You can find out about American alligators online at *http://animaldiversity.ummz.umich.edu* and *http://www.flmnh.ufl.edu/cnhc/csp_amis.htm*.

Investigate
Mental Math: What year did the alligator die? About how many sets of teeth might she have had?

1986

The Air Force orders two Boeing 747-200s to serve the needs of the President. Air Force One has 85 telephones, 19 television monitors, and 11 videocassette players. It can carry 70 passengers and 23 crew members. It flies at a cruising altitude of 35,000 feet and a cruising speed of 560 miles per hour. It can fly 7,140 miles without refueling.

Investigate
Write a math problem using the Air Force One data above.

JUNE 6
1985

Scientists at the University of California, Berkeley, confirm the existence of a black hole in the center of the Milky Way; this black hole is four million times greater than the mass of the Sun.

Investigate
First, compare the size of the Sun with the size of the Earth. What does this do to your conception of something four million times larger than the Sun?

1998

By completing a 25.2-mile marathon (his time is 4 hours, 1 minute, 8 seconds),

Houston oil executive Rick Worley breaks a world record by having competed in a marathon for the 75th consecutive week. (He's actually run 86 races, because some weeks he runs twice.)

Investigate
In what week in what year did Rick Worley run his first marathon in this sequence?

How many competitive miles did he run if each marathon was the same length as his 75th?

JUNE 7

570

Muhammad, future founder of the religion of Islam, is born.

Investigate
Mental Math: How many years ago was Muhammad born?

1896

George Harpo and Frank Samuelson leave New York City in a rowboat. They arrive at Scilly Isles, off the coast of England, 54 days later.

Investigate
Research the distance these men row. Compute the day they arrive at Scilly Isles.

JUNE 8

1909

Virginia Apgar is born. In 1952, Dr. Apgar develops a simple assessment by which doctors and nurses can evaluate the health of newborns immediately after they are born. This test allows less healthy babies to receive speedy help. At one minute of age and again at five minutes, a baby is evaluated for heart rate, respiration, muscle tone, and reflex response.

Investigate
Take your own pulse, and then chart the range of pulse rates in your classroom.

How many babies do you think are born each day in the United States? Estimate, then find out.

1786

The first commercially made ice cream is sold in New York City.

Investigate
Vanilla is the most popular flavor sold. Is this true for the students in your class? Poll students' favorite ice cream flavors and graph the results.

JUNE 9

1902

The first Automat, a restaurant serving food through windowed vending machines, opens in Philadelphia.

Investigate
How many different coin combinations (excluding pennies) can you use to buy a 65-cent Automat item?

1909

Twenty-two-year-old Alice Ramsey leaves New York City in an automobile, hoping to be the first woman to drive across America. A friend and two sisters-in-law travel with her but Alice does all the driving. The car's top speed is 43 miles per hour. Stops along the way include Buffalo, Chicago, Sioux City, Cheyenne, Salt Lake City, Reno, and Sacramento. Fifty-nine days later, Alice reaches San Francisco. Over the next seventy years, Alice drove across the United States thirty more times.

In 1999, Sue Mead and Tara Baukus Mello duplicate Alice's drive, but they do it in nine days.

1902
Philadelphia, Pennsylvania

Investigate

On what day does Alice arrive in San Francisco?

JUNE 10

1815

"I cannot live without books," Thomas Jefferson writes to his friend John Adams. Wanting to be able to locate any book in his voluminous collection instantly, Jefferson devises a classification system made up of 44 subjects. Jefferson later sells his books to the federal government and the Library of Congress uses this formula for 100 years.

Investigate

Devise a classification system for the books in your classroom library.

Determine the mathematics behind both the Dewey Decimal and the Library of Congress classification systems.

1944

Fifteen-year-old Joe Nuxhall takes the mound for the Cincinnati Reds, becoming the youngest person to play in the major leagues.

79

JUNE 11

1939

The king and queen of England, visiting President and Mrs. Franklin Roosevelt at their home on the Hudson River in New York, make gastronomic history by eating their first hot dogs. The *New York Times* records the event with a front-page head-line: "King Tries Hot Dog and Asks for More." The queen is baffled by just how to approach a hot dog and finally settles on using a knife and fork instead of following President Roosevelt's advice and just raising it to her mouth with her hand.

Investigate

According to a national poll, 7 percent of adults prefer hot dogs with nothing on them, 21 percent use just one topping, and 72 per-cent prefer multiple toppings. How do the preferences of the students in your class compare with these national averages?

1988

Adragon Eastwood De Mello, eleven years old, graduates from the University of California in Santa Cruz with a degree in mathematics.

Investigate

Mental Math: What year was Adragon born?

Subtracting 11 from 88 is easy. Devise a way that makes it easy to subtract 11 from 86, 16, or any other number.

JUNE 12

1967

The Russian space capsule *Venera* 4 is launched. It later reports a temperature on Venus of 536 degrees Fahrenheit. You can find out more information about the planets online at *http://pds.jpl.nasa.gov/planets* and *http://seds.lpl.arizona/edu/nineplanets/nineplanets/nineplanets.html*.

Investigate

Graph the relative "hotness" of the planets in our solar system.

1979

Bryan Allen pedals his 70-pound man-powered flyer, the *Gossamer Albatross*, into the air, crossing the English Channel as he cruises at 16 feet above the water. At a top speed of 10 miles per hour, the trip from Kent, England, to Cap Gris-Nex, France, takes him 2 hours, 49 minutes. Allen shares the prize money (100,000 pounds) offered November 30, 1977, for the first man-powered flight across the English Channel with the craft's designer.

The plane's designer then scales it down to three-fourths of its previous size—for solar-powered flight with a human pilot. The plane has 3,920 solar cells capable of pro-ducing 541 Watts of power. The first pilot is a thirteen-year-old boy who weighed 80 pounds. The official project pilot is Janice Brown, who weighs less than 100 pounds. She flew for a public demonstration on August 7, 1980—1.95 miles in 14 minutes, 21 seconds.

Investigate

Determine why there is so much emphasis on the weight of the pilots.

JUNE 13

1994

The Saskatchewan Seniors' Association, in Canada, finish the world's largest quilt. It measures 115 feet, $4\frac{1}{2}$ inches by 82 feet, 8 inches.

Investigate

With your classmates, collaborate on making a paper quilt using geometric shapes. Can you devise a symmetrical pattern?

1998

A football-sized rock weighing thirty-seven pounds slams into a Portales, New Mexico, art teacher's yard, burrowing a hole ten inches deep. Experts determine that it is a rare type of meteorite that can offer clues to the early days of our solar system. They think it might have broken off when two big space rocks collided 4.5 billion years ago.

Investigate

Compare the weight of the meteorite with the weight of a football. Estimate how many footballs it would take to equal the weight of the meteorite.

JUNE 14
1777

Congress adopts the 13-star-13-stripe U.S. flag, and the first Flag Day is celebrated.

Investigate

How many Flag Days have we celebrated since 1777?

1998

Tori Murden sets off from Nags Head, North Carolina, in her 23-foot boat, hoping to become the first woman to row across the Atlantic Ocean. She runs into Hurricane Danielle, which batters her boat with 30-foot waves and capsizes it 11 times. Finally, a merchant ship pulls Murden out of the water about 950 miles west of Brest, France, 85 days after she begins her journey.

Investigate

About how many miles did Murden row? About how many more days would she have needed to reach the French shore?

JUNE 15
1752

Benjamin Franklin flies a special kite made of silk handkerchiefs to prove that lightning is a form of electricity. This day is now observed as National Electricity Day.

Investigate

As a diversion, Franklin enjoyed creating "magic squares." He created a famous one measuring 16 × 16. You can start out with a 3 × 3 grid, arranging numbers 1 to 9 so that each row, column, and diagonal adds up to 15. Then, can you invent a magic square using other numbers?

1919

Piloting a Vickers-Vimy biplane, Captain John Alcock, from Great Britain, and Lieutenant Arthur Brown, from the United States, become the first people to fly nonstop across the Atlantic Ocean. They fly through fog and sleet, crash-landing in a bog in Ireland 16 hours, 12 minutes later. They fly 1,900 miles (3,040 kilometers).

Investigate

How fast was this plane traveling?

JUNE 16
1884

At Coney Island, in Brooklyn, New York, the first roller coaster opens. In December 1998, a coaster manufacturer advertised in a Palm Springs, California newspaper, offering to build a coaster for a private individual. All one needs are yard space of 165 feet by 50 feet and $1,999,999. The ride lasts one minute and the coaster car accommodates 11 passengers.

Coney Island, New York

Investigate

If 11 people agreed to build a private roller coaster together, how much money would each person need to contribute?

1987

Tom McClean starts out from Newfoundland, Canada, on his *second* attempt to row across the Atlantic Ocean.

Investigate

Create a poster displaying mathematical facts about the Atlantic Ocean. For example: How many miles does its average depth of 11,730 feet equal? How much of the U.S. land mass would be covered by its area of 33 million square miles?

JUNE 17

1898

Maurits Corneille Escher is born, in the Netherlands. Escher later becomes a graphic artist famous for his visual riddles—his "impossible" perspectives—which he achieves by manipulating the spatial aspects of geometry.

The official Escher Web site is *http://www.mcescher.com*. A great teaching site that shows how to make tesselations (geo-metric designs) is *http://www.iproject.com/escher/escherhome.html*.

Investigate

Celebrate Escher's birthday by creating your own tesselations.

1984

According to Sid Fleishman's *McBroom's Almanac*, "By actual count, 4,678,092,456,190,359,121 fireflies appeared on June 17. Folks needed sunglasses to step outside at night." *McBroom's Almanac* continues the tall-tale tradition of Paul Bunyan and Sally Ann Thunder Ann Whirlwind Crockett.

Investigate

Read a tall tale aloud and then create your own numerical and size exaggerations.

JUNE 18

1931

The first master's degree in city planning is awarded, by Harvard University.

Investigate

Give some examples of how mathematics is necessary in planning a city.

Invite a member of the local city planning commission or zoning board to speak to your class.

1988

Fourteen members of the class of 1988 of Hanover High School, in Hanover, New Hampshire, complete 189 hours, 49 minutes of leapfrogging. In this time they leapfrog 888.1 miles.

In 1991, 14 students from a dorm at Stanford University leapfrogged for 244 hours, 43 minutes, or 996.2 miles.

How many days does each of these time spans equal?

JUNE 19

1623

Blaise Pascal, French scientist and philosopher, credited with inventing a calculating machine, developing the theory of probability, and contributing to the theory of differential calculus, is born.

Provocative visuals of Pascal's triangle are online at *http://www.angelfire.com/il/peterw311/index.html*.

Investigate

What are the possible outcomes when one coin is tossed? When two coins are tossed? The number of ways these coins can land can be shown in a triangular arrangement (Pascal's Triangle), starting with a 1 on top:

                1

1 coin   1 1 (h or t)

2 coins   1 2 1 (hh, ht, th, tt)

3 coins 1 3 3 1 (hhh, hht, hth, thh, htt, tht, tth, ttt)

Use this triangular pattern to figure out the outcomes when four and five coins are tossed. (Add the sum of each row of the triangle and discuss the patterns you see.)

1978

Garfield, the lasagna-loving, coffee-guzzling cat created by cartoonist Jim Davis, makes his debut, appearing in 41 newspapers. Twenty years later, he appears in 2,550 newspapers around the world. Garfield is the largest latex balloon to appear in Macy's Thanksgiving Day Parade, in New York City. At 61 feet long and 35 feet wide, Garfield holds 18,907 cubic feet of helium and air.

This Garfield's skin is made of nearly 450 pounds of nylon, coated on both sides with urethane and heat sealed so air won't leak out. Garfield also has his own Web site: *http://www.garfield.com*.

Investigate

If Jim Davis has drawn a cartoon every day, beginning on June 19, 1978, how many cartoons has he drawn so far?

JUNE 20

1838

James Audubon completes the last plate of his great work, *The Birds of America*. His goal has been to paint all the species of American birds. He has traveled around the country looking for birds and painting them. After eighteen years he has painted 435 life-size illustrations. Subscribers to his collection pay $1,000 each. At an auction in 1977, a copy of Audubon's original work sells for $400,000.

Children at the Audubon School have created a site: *http://www.methacton.k12.pa.us/audubon/mill_grove.html*.

Investigate

How many bird paintings, on average, did Audubon complete each year?

1988

The U.S. Libertas Scavolini basketball team sets up the longest table on record, in Pesaro, Italy. The table is 10,072 feet long.

Investigate

How many people do you think can sit down at this table? Explain how you arrived at your answer and explain why this answer makes sense.

How long a table would you need to seat everyone in the class? in the school?

JUNE 21

Today is the summer solstice. Imagine you are standing at the North Pole. The Arctic Ocean is 6 or 7 feet under the snow; it is 13,000 feet deep, and the water temperature is about 29 degrees Fahrenheit. You are standing 440 miles from the nearest piece of land, the tiny island of Oodaaq, off the coast of northern Greenland. You stand in each of the world's 24 time zones simultaneously. The sun is making a flat 360-degree orbit exactly $23\frac{1}{2}$ degrees above the horizon.

Investigate
Check in your local newspaper to see how many hours of daylight there will be on this day. Compare this with yesterday; with the longest day of the year.

1994

David Bogen, of La Canada, California, receives a patent for a paper-clip holder. On July 12, 1992, sixty students at the Nanyang Technological University, in Singapore, achieve the record for making a paper-clip chain—they use 190,400 paper clips. It takes them 5 hours, 35 minutes.

Investigate
Assuming they use 2-inch paper clips, how long is the paper-clip chain the students produce? How much more difficult would it be to solve this problem if the clips were $\frac{5}{16}''$ or $1\frac{3}{8}''$ long?

JUNE 22
1909

The first transcontinental automobile race ends, at Seattle, Washington. It began on June 1, in New York City.

Investigate
How long would it take a car to make this trip at the average speed maintained by participants in the Indianapolis 500?

1940

Ice cream maker J. F. McCullough, who thinks ice cream tastes better when it is soft, opens the first Dairy Queen, in Joliet, Illinois. Fifty years later, there were 5,200 Dairy Queens in the United States.

Investigate
How many Dairy Queens, on average, were there in each state in 1990?

Propose a plan outlining the optimal locations for 5,200 Dairy Queens.

JUNE 23
1868

Christopher Sholes patents the typewriter.

Investigate
Mental Math: How old is the typewriter?

1998

Michael Olowokandi, of Pacific University, is selected as the number one draft pick in the National Basketball Association—even though he's played in only 55 games in his life. The Los Angeles Clippers feel confident they can teach someone 7 feet, 1 inch tall how to play the game. The second draft pick is 6 feet, 1 inch tall.

Investigate
Draw two figures on a sheet of paper, one 7 feet, 1 inch tall and one your own height. Explain how you measured.

JUNE 24
1938

Congress passes the Food, Drug, and Cosmetic Act, which requires that

1989
Luling, Texas

ingredients be listed on product labels.

Investigate
Along with your classmates, bring in a label from a popular food. As a class examine these labels for content and nutrition. How does each contribute (or not contribute) to the minimum daily requirement of vitamins and minerals?

1989

In Luling, Texas, Lee Wheelis spits a watermelon seed 68 feet, $9\frac{3}{8}$ inches.

Investigate
There are other mathematical things you can do with a watermelon, such as estimating its length, width, distance around, area of the rind, and number of seeds. Then see how close your estimates were. Or, have a class contest with teams making estimates in each category.

JUNE 25
1798

At age 19, Peter Mark Roget earns an M.D. degree from the University of Edinburgh.

His fascination with classifying ideas leads to the work we now know as *Roget's Thesaurus*. You can access the most recent edition of *Roget's Thesaurus* online at *http://www .thesaurus.com*.

Investigate
Suggest probable categories for a system of classifying ideas in mathematics.

1852

Cecilia McMillen Adams keeps a diary of her family's journey from Illinois to Oregon. She provides grim proof of the hardship of the journey. On this date her diary notes: "Passed 7 graves . . . made 14 miles." The next day she records: "Passed 8 graves . . . made 15 miles." On June 30: "Passed 10 graves . . . made 22 miles."

Investigate
Estimate how long it took Cecilia's family to make their trip.

JUNE 26
1819

The bicycle was patented by W. K. Clarkson, Jr., of New York City.

Investigate
Take measurements of your bicycle—the height of its seat, the diameter of its wheels, its length, and so on—and compare your data with classmates.

1895

Annie Londonberry leaves Boston on her bicycle; she is the first woman to attempt to bicycle around the world. The women's record for cycling across America is held by Seana Hogan, who did it in 9 days, 8 hours, 54 minutes.

Investigate

Make a reasonable guess about how many hours Hogan rode a day. Then estimate her average speed.

JUNE 27

1917

A bill establishing daylight saving time, sponsored by the National Daylight Saving Association, is passed by the U.S. Senate.

Investigate

Discuss the way time zones work across the country.

You can access time on CNN's world map: *http://www.cnn.com/weather/worldtime*. For U.S. Naval observatory master clock time, the official timekeeper, see *http://tycho .usno.navy.mil/time.html*. For the world clock, see *http://www.timeanddate.com/worldclock/*.

1974

Dave Kunst arrives home in Wasica, Minnesota, the first person to walk around the world. In 1969, after watching men land on the moon, he decided he wanted to do something nobody had ever done. On June 20, 1970, Dave and his brother headed toward the Atlantic Ocean with a mule. The brothers flew from New York to Portugal and picked up another mule there. The brothers were shot in Afghanistan, and Dave's brother died. But Dave kept walking, for a total of 14,452 miles.

Investigate

If Dave took 31 steps per 100 feet, figure out how many steps he took in his round-the-world trek.

About how many steps do you take every 100 feet?

JUNE 28

1921

Bridge builder Joseph Strauss submits his finished plans for the Golden Gate Bridge to city officials in San Francisco. Some people worry that the bridge will spoil the natural beauty of the landscape. After spending a dozen years convincing people that the bridge should be built, Strauss noted, "The value of an idea depends not only on the sweat you put into thinking it up, but also on the sweat you put into getting people to accept it." The Golden Gate Bridge is famous not only for its beauty but also for its span of 4,200 feet. You can visit the Golden Gate Bridge online at *http://www.mcn.org /goldengate/*.

Investigate

Measure the longest corridor in your school and figure out how many times the corridor could be laid end to end on the span of the Golden Gate.

1988

At the Kibbutz Ha'on collective farm, in Israel, a two-year-old ostrich lays an egg weighing 5.1 pounds, a record. The elephant bird, the largest bird ever to have existed, stood 9 to 11 feet tall, weighed almost 1,000 pounds, and laid 20-pound eggs.

For more ostrich information, see *http://animaldiversity.ummz.umich.edu/accounts /struthio/s._camelus* and *http://www.science .nus.edu.sg/~webdbs/bird/livebird/ostrich*.

Investigate

Chicken eggs weigh between 21 ounces and 30 ounces per dozen. How many chicken eggs would weigh the same as the 5.1-pound ostrich egg?

How many people do you think an omelet made from the record-setting ostrich egg would feed?

1921
Plan for
Golden Gate
Bridge

SPAN: 4,200 feet

JUNE 29

1985

The Crayola 64-pack goes on the market. It contains 13 varieties of blue: blue, cerulean, sky, aquamarine, cornflower, teal, blue green, midnight, turquoise, blue violet, navy, cadet, and periwinkle.

Investigate
About what percent of the Crayola 64-pack are blue crayons?

Invent five different shades of green, giving each shade a name. Keep track of your "recipes," carefully recording the amounts of blue and yellow you use for each hue.

1985

Bob Brown, of Boston, breaks the yo-yo endurance record, having maintained a

bounce for 121 hours. Check out some yo-yo tips online at *http://pages.nyu.edu?~tqm3413/yoyo* (select M, then select *Tomer Moscovich*) and *http://www.pd.net/yoyo*, which is the official site of the American Yo-Yo Association.

Investigate
How many days did Bob Brown keep his yo-yo bouncing?

JUNE 30

1964

Accepting the Caldecott Medal for *Where the Wild Things Are*, Maurice Sendak tells of receiving a letter from a seven-year-old boy in which the boy asked, "How much does it cost to get to where the wild things are? If it is not too expensive, my sister and I want to spend the summer there." Sendak says he did not answer these questions: "I have no doubt that sooner or later they will find their way, free of charge."

Investigate

If Max, the central character in this book, was born in 1964, how old would he be today?

1991

After Francis Johnson's death, the residents of Darwin, Minnesota, decide to give the 8.7-ton ball of twine that sat in his front yard for decades a place of prominence: they move it downtown. Johnson began saving twine in 1950 and by 1978 his ball was 12 feet, 9 inches in diameter, had a circumference of 40 feet, and weighed 11 tons.

Investigate

As a class, start winding string or rubber bands into a ball. Monitor its growth. Once a week, measure the circumference and weigh it. See if a pattern emerges.

J U L Y

JULY 1

1874

The Philadelphia Zoological Society opens the first U.S. zoo. On this day 3,000 visitors pay 25 cents (adults) or 10 cents (children) to see the 1,000 animals in the zoo. You can visit zoos online at *http://www.zoos.com* and *http://www. zoonet.org*.

Investigate
If there were two children visitors for every one adult visitor, how much money did the zoo take in on opening day? What if there were two children for every two adults? Or, three children for every two adults? Figure out a way to compute the money for any combination of children and adults that totals 3,000 visitors.

1963

The United States Post Office begins using zip codes. (Unlike telephone area codes, which have no relationship to geographical location, zip codes do have a pattern.) Check *http://www.usps.gov/postofc*.

Investigate
Make a zip code map of the United States, putting in the zip codes of state capitals. Then look for and identify patterns.

Using five numbers, there are ten thousand possible zip codes, from 00000 to 99999. Explain why this is true.

1928

A hailstone weighing 1.5 pounds, with a 5.5-inch diameter and 17-inch circumference, falls to earth near Potter, Nebraska. This is the hailstone record until 1970, when a hailstone with a 17.5-inch circumference hits Coffeyville, Kansas.

Investigate

Create a paper "hailstone" with the dimensions of the one that fell in Nebraska. Lay an ice cube next to it; about how many times bigger is the paper "hailstone" than the ice cube?

Try measuring the circumference of a few objects. Start with your head.

1982

Larry Water sits in a lawn chair to which are attached four clusters of helium-filled weather balloons (42 in all). Each balloon is inflated to about 7 feet in diameter and can lift a weight of about 12 pounds. The balloons carry his chair to a height of 16,500 feet (it rises at 800 feet per minute). Later, he is fined $1,500 by

1982
Larry Water flies an "unairworthy machine."

the Federal Aviation Administration for flying an "unairworthy machine."

Investigate
Mental Math: How much weight were Larry's balloons capable of lifting?

How many miles are 16,500 feet?

JULY 3
1898

Captain Joshua Slocum sails into the Fairhaven, Massachusetts, harbor aboard *The Spray*, becoming the first man to circumnavigate the world alone. His sloop is 36 feet, 9 inches long; 14 feet, 2 inches wide; and 4 feet, 2 inches deep. He sailed from Boston Harbor on April 24, 1895, and has traveled 46,000 miles.

Investigate
How many days did Slocum's trip take?

Find out how far an adult you know travels to and from work each day, and then figure out how many miles this comes to in a year of workdays.

1998

Author Kevin Anderson makes a bid for *The Guinness Book of World Records* in a new category—largest book signing by a single author (one book per person). Anderson signs 2,000 copies of a novelization he wrote of an original L. Ron Hubbard story.

Investigate
Estimate how long it would take you to sign your name 2,000 times. Then figure out a way to check your estimate without actually writing your name 2,000 times.

JULY 4
1776

The Declaration of Independence is signed, in Philadelphia, Pennsylvania. You can access a copy of the actual document online at *http://lcweb.loc.gov* or *http://www.nara.gov/exhall/charters/declaration/decmain.html*.

Investigate
Mental Math: How old is the Declaration of Independence?

1971

Koko the gorilla is born at the San Francisco Zoo. She is taught to communicate in American Sign Language. In 1998, Koko answers questions on America Online.

The Gorilla Foundation has a Web site featuring Koko, including answers to frequently asked questions: *http://www.koko.org*.

Investigate
Mental Math: How old was Koko when she went online?

What are the 100 most important words you'd want to teach someone learning American Sign Language?

JULY 5
1784

Thomas Jefferson ends his period of service as minister to the French Government. While in France, Thomas Jefferson has acquired 28 saucepans, 4 waffle irons, and a recipe for ice cream that begins, "2 bottles of good cream, 5 yolks of eggs, and $\frac{1}{2}$ pound sugar . . ."

Investigate
What percentage of your classmates have waffle irons at home? Take a poll and find out.

How many saucepans do your classmates have at home? Poll and gauge the results. (A saucepan holds one quart of liquid.) How does Jefferson's collection compare with the number of saucepans in your home?

1996

Dolly, a cloned sheep, is born in a small village near Edinburgh. A cloned offspring has the same genetic makeup as its parent. (Normal offspring share the genetic makeup of both parents.)

Investigate

Examine a chart detailing how eye color is inherited. What are the odds that a blue-eyed mother and a brown-eyed father will have a blue-eyed child? a brown-eyed child? Do the odds change if the eye color of the mother and father are reversed?

JULY 6

1785

The Continental Congress adopts the decimal system of money, with the dollar as a unit. The smallest unit is a copper coin "of which two hundred shall pass for one dollar."

Investigate

What decimal part of a dollar does each coin presently in use in the United States represent?

Discuss the logic of adopting a decimal measuring system.

1858

Lyman Reed Blake, of Abington, Massachusetts, obtains a patent for a shoe-stitching machine.

Investigate

Who has the biggest foot in your school?

Trace one of your feet on centimeter-squared paper and figure its area and length. Mark your shoe size on your cut-out foot. Compare with your classmates. Does a larger area mean a larger shoe size? Does a longer foot affect shoe size? What can you discover?

JULY 7

1940

TWA initiates flights between New York and Los Angeles. Planes fly at a cruising altitude of 19,000 feet, and the flight time is 13 hours. Planes today fly at a cruising altitude of 30,000 feet. At greater heights there is less air resistance, so planes can fly faster.

Investigate

What was the average speed per hour of a plane in 1940? What is the average per-hour speed of a plane today?

How long does it take a passenger plane to fly from New York to Los Angeles today? From Los Angeles to New York? Why are these two estimated flying times different?

1997

Residents of Tower, Minnesota, are surprised by the morning temperature—24 degrees Fahrenheit. Weather information is available online at *http://www.WHNT19.com /kidwx* and *http://www.usatoday.com/weather /wfront.htm.*

Investigate

Consult an almanac and check typical temperatures on this date across the country.

JULY 8

1911

Nan Jane Aspinwall arrives in New York City on horseback, carrying a letter to the mayor from the mayor of San Francisco, where she began her journey. She left San Francisco on September 1, 1910, and has spent 108 days during this period traveling 4,500 miles.

Investigate

How many months was Aspinwall in transit?

Approximately how many miles did she cover each day she traveled?

1988

USA *Today* reports that there are 67 billionaires in the United States. John Paul Getty once said, "If you can count your money you aren't a billionaire."

Investigate

If a person wanted to spend a billion dollars in one year, how much would he or she have to spend each day?

JULY 9

1872

J. F. Blondel, of Thomaston, Maine, patents the donut cutter.

Investigate

Find out the favorite donut variety of each student in your class and display this information graphically.

Design an ad proclaiming the benefits of a snack food with a hole in the middle.

1936

The thermometer hits 106 degrees Fahrenheit in New York's Central Park. It is

1872 — The donut cutter is patented.

the first day of a ten-day heat wave that breaks records across the United States and Canada. Temperature data is available online at *http://www.WHNT19.com/kidwx* and *http://www.usatoday.com/weather/wfront.htm*.

Investigate

What is the hottest it has ever been in July in your area?

Graph the high temperature each day for the month of July. Then, at the end of the month, figure the range, mean, median, and mode.

JULY 10

1866

Edson Clark, of Northampton, Massachusetts, receives patent number 56,180, for the indelible pencil. Today the Eberhard Faber Pencil Division, in Lewisburg, Tennessee, makes 32,400 pencils every hour.

Investigate

You've heard the expression "You're worth your weight in gold." What is your weight in pencils? How long would it take the Eberhard Faber Pencil Division to make enough pencils to equal the combined weight of everyone in your classroom?

1913

The thermometer hits a record 134 degrees Fahrenheit in Death Valley, California. This is the highest temperature ever recorded in the United States. Death Valley's 140-mile-long-6-mile-wide area has the highest summer temperatures in the world, averaging 116 degrees in July. It is also the driest place in the country, with a yearly average rainfall of 1.63 inches.

Investigate

What is the average rainfall in your area in a year? Make a month-by-month graph to show the information.

What is the average high temperature in your area each month? Make a month-by-month graph to show the information.

1962

Telstar 1 is launched, initiating the first trans-Atlantic exchange of live television pictures via relay stations in the United States, England, and France. All the colors you see on a television screen are mixtures of red, yellow, and blue light. Most colors can be mixed from three primary colors, red, yellow, and blue, because that's the way our eyes work. At the back of the eye are three different kinds of cone cells, and each kind is sensitive to different wavelengths of light.

Investigate

In teams, conduct color-mixing experiments with red, yellow, and blue paint or food coloring, keeping a record of what proportions produce which colors. Another team should be able to produce the same colors by following your team's instructions.

Mixing red and yellow makes orange. If you make three batches as described below, how would the orange mixtures compare?

2 parts red	1 part yellow
3 parts red	2 parts yellow
4 parts red	1 part yellow

JULY 11

1975

A huge army of 6,000 life-size terra-cotta warriors is unearthed by Chinese archaeologists near the ancient capital of Xian. These soldiers have been guarding the tomb of the first Qin emperor for more than 2,000 years.

Investigate

How many years has it been since Qin Shi Huangdi's death, in 206 B.C.?

1998

Shelley Taylor-Smith wins the 28.5-mile Manhattan Island Marathon (a swim around Manhattan) for the fifth time. In 1995, she set the record for both men and women by completing the swim in 5 hours, 45 minutes, 25 seconds. Ms. Taylor-Smith's swimming strength and speed have roots in her childhood: she had scoliosis and had to wear a back brace. The water was one of the few places she could move around without it, and she spent a lot of time in the pool.

Investigate

Mental Math: Estimate how many miles Shelley Taylor-Smith averages an hour.

JULY 12

1933

A minimum wage of 40 cents an hour is established in the United States.

Investigate

How many times more than 40 cents is today's minimum wage?

1960

Etch-a-Sketch goes on sale. Invented in France by Arthur Granjean, who calls it "L'Ecran Magique" (The Magic Screen), the device is marketed in the United States by the Ohio Art Company. The executive model sells for $3,750. Its silver case has knobs decorated with the customer's choice of topaz or sapphire gems.

Investigate

Draw a picture using the Etch-a-Sketch parameters: that is, start out with one straight line, and the only way you can change that line is to move it at a right angle.

1983

Andy, a polar bear at the Atlanta Zoo, is given his own ice machine. He needs help in the Atlanta summer because his natural habitat is at the top of the world in the icy Arctic region. In the wild, a polar bear's paws are important in catching its preferred meal of seal. A paw weighs 25 pounds and measures $1\frac{1}{2}$ feet by 1 foot.

Investigate

Draw a rectangle $1\frac{1}{2}$ feet by 1 ft on several pieces of graph paper taped together. Then trace your own foot on a separate piece of graph paper. How many of your feet can fit in the space of one polar bear paw? What percentage or fraction of the polar bear's paw is your foot?

1944

Erno Rubik, future inventor of the Rubik's Cube, is born.

Investigate

Solve the Rubik's Cube puzzle (or a similar type of mathematical puzzle). Then write about how you went about it. Did you use trial and error? Did your organize your efforts in some way?

Entering "Rubik's Cube" on Yahoo search produces a variety of Web sites with interesting patterns.

Andy gets his own ice machine.

**1983
Atlanta, Georgia**

JULY 14

1868

Alvin Fellows, of New Haven, Connecticut, receives a patent for a tape measure enclosed in a circular case with a spring click lock to hold the tape at any desired point.

Investigate

Measure the length of ten items. For each, estimate first. Then write a statement about how the sizes of the items compare with one another.

1992

A king-size flag made by Humphrey's Flag Company, of Pottstown, Pennsylvania, is unfurled in Washington, D.C. The flag measures 505 feet by 255 feet and weighs 1.36 tons.

Investigate

A square that measures one foot on a side has the area of one square foot. What is the area of the king-size flag? How does the area of the flag compare to the area of a football field?

JULY 15

1960

The New York World-Telegram reports that the average office worker will earn a lifetime income of $200,000 (forty years at $5,000 per year).

Investigate

What might be the lifetime income of someone beginning office work today?

1983

Ending in Washington, D.C., the place he started, Robert Sweetgall finishes his run around the perimeter of the United States. He has run 10,608 miles.

Investigate

Plan your own "around the United States" run, starting from your home. About how many miles will you run? How does this compare with Sweetgall's 10,608?

JULY 16

1935

The Park-O-Meter, the first automatic parking meter, is installed, in Oklahoma City. The parking fee is 5 cents.

Investigate

Assume the parking fee in your town is 85 cents an hour and parking meters take quarters, dimes, and nickels. Figure out all possible coin combinations for one hour's parking.

1998

Benoit Lecomte, a 31-year-old transplanted Frenchman from Austin, Texas, wades into the water off Cape Cod to begin his 73-day-3,700-mile swim across the Atlantic to France. His routine will be to swim three hours, take a two-hour break on a 40-foot sloop that accompanies him, then swim for another three hours. Later Lecomte said that during his swim he lived minute to minute, never thinking about the next day or even the next hour. Most days, he used 7,000 to 8,000 calories.

Investigate

How many miles did Lecomte average a day?

Design a number of daily menus that will add up to 8,000 calories.

JULY 17

1874

Rocky Mountain locusts begin to swarm over Nebraska. The swarm sticks around for ten days and expands to cover an area of 198,600 square miles. Experts estimate that the swarm contains 12.5 trillion insects, with a total weight of about 27.5 million tons.

Investigate
How long would it take you to count to 12 trillion if you can say each number in half a second? How would using powers of ten help?

http://www.ccsf.caltech.edu/~roy/dataquan offers a chart of data powers of ten. *Powers of Ten* by Philip and Phylis Morrison offers a wonderful pictorial expression of this concept.

1968
The Beatles's feature-length cartoon, *Yellow Submarine*, premieres at the London Pavilion.

Investigate
Poll your classmates to see who has seen the movie. Graph the results.

JULY 18
1882
Louisville pitcher Tony Mullane becomes the first major-leaguer to pitch right-handed and left-handed in the same game. Although about 90 percent of people are right-handed, some famous people, including George Bush and Bill Clinton, are lefties.

Investigate
What is the percentage of left-handers in your class? How does it compare with the national average?

1991
Marty Doyle gives away 573 books at his Traveler Restaurant, located off Interstate 84 at the Connecticut-Massachusetts border. He advertises the restaurant as the only

literary roadside restaurant. To keep up his inventory, Doyle goes to auctions and estate sales, buying 50 tons of books a year, sometimes 10,000 at a time.

Investigate
Would 10,000 books fit in your classroom? In your school library?

JULY 19
1903
Maurice Garin, a 32-year-old French chimney sweep, wins the first Tour de France bicycle race. The six-stage race began in Paris on July 1 and covers 1,509 miles (2,428 kilometers). The route goes through Lyons, Marseilles, Toulouse, Bordeaux, and Nantes.

Investigate
How many miles did Garin average a day?

1994
Susan Montgomery Williams, of Fresno, California, blows a bubble-gum bubble with a diameter of 23 inches.

Investigate
Measure the diameter of several balls—a basketball, soccer ball, tennis ball, etc. How much larger than each is the bubble-gum bubble? Represent your findings on a poster.

JULY 20
1919
Edmund Hillary, who later becomes the first person to climb Mount Everest, is born in Auckland, New Zealand. When asked why he climbed Everest, he replied, "We climbed because nobody climbed it before." Altitudes above 26,000 feet affect climbers' minds and bodies. They don't want to eat,

drink, or put their boots on. Sometimes they cover the terrain at an average of just 12 feet per minute.

Investigate
How many feet do you walk in a minute at an average gait?

1986

Teiichi Igarashi, at the age of 99 years, 302 days, climbs to the 12,388-foot peak of Mt. Fuji.

Investigate
Mental Math: Estimate how many miles high Mt. Fugi is.

JULY 21
1812

Sculptor Giuseppi Franzoni submits an estimate of the cost for carving six female figures to be used as columns to support the back of the public gallery of the Capitol in Washington, D.C., to Benjamin Henry Latrobe, the architect who designed the figures. The cost for each figure varies with the degree of ornateness. The goddess of war, $125; of agriculture, $150; of commerce, $150; of science, $175; of wisdom, $200; of art, $400.

Investigate
Prepare Franzoni's total bill.

1985

After searching for sixteen years, treasure hunter Mel Fisher finds the wreck of the Spanish galleon *Nestra Senora de Atocha*, valued at 400 million dollars. The galleon sank off the coast of Key West, Florida, in 1622.

This and other shipwrecks are described online at *http://www.melfisher.org*.

Investigate
Mental Math: How long did the galleon lie in the ocean undiscovered?

JULY 22
1962

Mariner 1 is launched from Cape Canaveral, Florida, on a journey to provide the first close-up view of the planet Venus. Four minutes after takeoff, the spaceship crashes into the Atlantic. A minus sign has mistakenly been omitted from a computer program, and the computer gave the spaceship the wrong instructions. The missing minus sign costs the U.S. space program $18.5 million.

Investigate
Look at an outdoor thermometer. How far apart are −20 degrees and +20 degrees?

Invent a math problem in which the minus sign is crucial.

JULY 23

1715

The first lighthouse in America is authorized. The conical masonry tower is erected by the Province of Massachusetts on Little Brewster Island, at the entrance to Boston Harbor. It is initially illuminated with firelight; the first fire is kindled on Sept. 14, 1716. A levy of a penny per ton is placed on all incoming and outgoing vessels.

Investigate

Prepare a bill for the *Disney Magic*, at 83,000 tons the third-largest cruise ship in the world, if it is charged 1716 rates when it enters and leaves Boston Harbor.

1921

Edward Gourdin becomes the first person to long-jump more than 25 feet.

Investigate

What is the current record for the long jump? How much has it increased since 1921?

JULY 24

1911

High in the Andes mountains of Peru, U.S. archaeologist Hiram Bingham discovers the ruins of Machu Picchu, the last capital of the ancient Inca civilization. The site, long known to Peruvians, had been kept secret from Europeans. This ancient fortress city contains five square miles of terraces, with over 3,000 steps linking its many levels.

Investigate

Keep track of the steps on buildings in your community until you reach 3,000. List the buildings and the number of steps for each.

1996

Kraft Foods and Lender's Bagels, in Mattoon, Illinois, make a bagel weighing 563 pounds and measuring about 59 inches in diameter, 185 inches around the circumference, and 12 inches thick.

Investigate

Measure the diameter, circumference, and thickness of various round foods: Oreos, donuts, and so on. Look for patterns in your measurements.

Is this over-size bagel proportionate with a regular-size one?

JULY 25

1983

A temperature of −128.6 degrees Fahrenheit is recorded at Vostok, Antarctica. Antarctica, the fifth-largest continent, has an area of 5,500,000 square miles. More than 95 percent of it is covered by ice. The most famous residents are Emperor penguins. You can find out more about Antarctica online at *http://www.theice.org*.

Investigate

Mental Math: How does this temperature compare with average low temperatures where you live?

1992

A line of 1,724,000 quarters is laid at the Atlanta Marriott Marquis Hotel by members of the National Exchange Club.

Investigate

What is the dollar value of these quarters?

How long is this line of quarters?

If your school were going to make a collection of one million items, how many items would each student need to bring?

JULY 26
1775

The Second Continental Congress appoints Benjamin Franklin the first postmaster general. Today, the U.S. Postal Service delivers 200 pieces of junk mail every second.

Investigate
How much would it cost to give everybody in the class a first-class stamp?

1985

The Soviet research ship *Mikhail Somov* and its crew are freed from the Antarctic ice after having been trapped for 133 days. You can visit the Antarctic online at *http://www.theice.org*.

Investigate
On what day did the ship become trapped?

JULY 27
1909

Orville Wright, one of the famous Wright Brothers, along with his brother, Wilbur, sets a record for the longest airplane flight. Testing the Army's first airplane over Fort Myer, Virginia, Wright keeps it aloft for 1 hour, 12 minutes, and 40 seconds. He is so tired from the experience that he crash-lands the plane, but he and his passenger are OK.

Investigate
How far do commercial jets fly today in 1 hour, 12 minutes, and 40 seconds? Research different airplanes and make a poster presenting what you find out.

1940

Bugs Bunny makes his debut, in A *Wild Hare*.

Investigate
Conduct a poll of your classmates' favorite cartoon characters. Graph the information.

JULY 28
1896

The community of Miami, Florida, is incorporated. The city has a population of 260. Today, the city of Miami area boasts a population of around 365,000.

Investigate
Mental Math: How long ago was Miami, Florida, incorporated?

How many times larger is the population of Miami today than in 1896?

Research the population of your town or city when it was first established and the population today. How many times larger or smaller is the population today?

1954

An unnamed English collector pays 7,000 dollars for a painting titled *Waterlily Pond and Path by the Water*, one of six paintings Claude Monet did in 1900 of his water garden, in Giverny. The painting hung in the collector's house until the summer of 1998, when Sotheby's sold it for 33 million dollars. One reason the painting is considered so valuable is that the other five water garden paintings are in museums.

Investigate
What percent profit did the collector earn from the sale?

**1954
From $7,000 to $33,000,000**

JULY 29

1914

The first transcontinental telephone service is inaugurated when two people hold a conversation between New York and San Francisco.

Investigate
What does it cost to make a three-minute call from New York to San Francisco?

1940

John Sigmund begins a 292-mile nonstop swim in the Mississippi River, from St. Louis to Caruthersville, Missouri. It takes him 89 hours, 40 minutes. In 1930, Fred Newton swam 1,826 miles of the Mississippi, from near Minneapolis, Minnesota, to New Orleans, Louisiana. He was in the water 742 hours.

Investigate
How many days are 742 hours?

JULY 30

1993

CharLee Torre, elephant-keeper at the Lowry Park Zoo, in Tampa, Florida, who has been on the job for just six months, is killed by Tillie, a four-ton Asian elephant. Tillie grabs Torre with her trunk, throws her to the ground, and stomps on her. Experts say Torre had not received enough training. Elephants are responsible for more keeper deaths than any other animal. About one elephant-keeper out of six hundred in zoos and circuses in the United States and Canada is killed every year. Statistically, elephant-keeping is the most dangerous profession in the country—deadlier than police work. That said, only 3 percent of the elephants in North America have been involved in human fatalities.

Investigate
Compare the weight of a 120-pound keeper with that of a four-ton elephant.

JULY 31

1792

Construction starts on the first building in the United States to be used solely by the government—the U.S. Mint, in Philadelphia. The word *mint* is derived from the temple of Juno Moneta, in Rome, where silver coins were made in 269 B.C. The current mint in Philadelphia is the fourth building constructed on that site; it opened in 1969 and occupies 500,000 square feet of space.

Investigate
Examine 100 pennies; what percentage were minted in Philadelphia?

1918

The first complete set of dishes made especially for the White House, ordered by President Woodrow Wilson, is delivered. The set features the seal of the President of the United States and has been made in Trenton, New Jersey, by the Lenox Company. It consists of 1,700 dishes. The China Room in the White House can be visited online at *http://www.whitehouse.gov*.

Investigate
How many people might this set serve?

1942

The Women's Auxiliary Voluntary Emergency Service (WAVES) is created by legislation signed by U.S. President Franklin D. Roosevelt. The members of the WAVES are part of the U.S. Navy.

Investigate
Research what percentage of Navy personnel today are women.

A U G U S T

AUGUST 1

1790

The first United States census is completed. The population is four million. You can contact the Census Bureau online at *http://www.census.gov*.

Investigate
Consult an almanac or the Census Bureau online to discover the current U.S. population. How many times larger is today's population?

Find out how many U.S. cities now have a population of more than four million. Is there a pattern to where these cities are located?

1893

Henry Perky and William Ford, of Watertown, New York, receive a patent for making shredded wheat biscuits.

Investigate
Bring to class an empty box of your favorite cereal. Make sure the price is on the box (write it on if it isn't printed there). Examine it in relation to the boxes brought in by your classmates. What are the best and worst buys?

AUGUST 2

1776

This day marks the formal signing of the Declaration of Independence. Today at the

National Archives Building in Washington, D.C., each page of the original document is protected in a glass and bronze case, filled with inert helium. More than 1,000,000 people view the document each year. One hundred and ninety-three years after the document is signed, one of sixteen known copies sells for $464,000.

Investigate

Who should get the money from the sale? Descendents of Thomas Jefferson, who wrote most of the document? Descendents of the members of the Continental Congress who signed it? Relatives of the closed bookstore where it was found? The person who found it? Should anyone get money from a document that belonged to the government?

1909

The Lincoln-head penny is first minted. This is the first U.S. coin to depict a real person.

Investigate

There is a perennial shortage. Some people say pennies are a nuisance and should be eliminated. Prepare a convincing argument for eliminating or keeping the penny.

AUGUST 3

1492

Under the leadership of Christopher Columbus, the *Nina*, the *Pinta*, and the *Santa Maria* set sail from Palos, Spain, searching for a new route to the East Indies. 792 hours later, traveling at an average speed of 4 miles per hour, the ships reach land at the Bahamas. The *Santa Maria*, Columbus's flagship, was about 80 feet long and 23 feet wide, and it carried a crew of 40.

Investigate

About how many days did the trip take? Mark the *Santa Maria*'s dimensions on the

playground, and have 40 people stand within the space.

1998

The *Boston Globe* points out that 14 percent of the country's 50 million pager users are teenagers. When paging each other, they often dial in numeric codes instead of a return phone number. The most widely used message is 143, meaning "I love you" (the digits signify the number of letters in each word of the affectionate phrase).

Investigate

About how many pager users are teenagers?

AUGUST 4

1735

John Peter Zenger, publisher of the *New York Weekly Journal*, is found innocent on a charge of seditious libel. He had printed criticism of the colonial governor in his paper. We now celebrate this as Freedom of the Press Day.

Investigate

Mental Math: How many years ago did the courts strike this important blow for a free press?

1959

U.S. Air Force Lt. Col. William Rankis is forced to bail out of his jet at 47,000 feet over Virginia, above a heavy thunderstorm. He falls 10,000 feet before opening his chute. Then the storm tosses him up and down. He lands 40 minutes later, 65 miles from where he bailed out.

Average-sized skydivers fall approximately 320 to 450 meters (1050 to 1480 feet) every five seconds, reaching 190 to 240 kilometers per hour (120 to 150 miles

1959
10,000 feet
over Virginia

per hour). Usually skydivers free-fall from 20 to 60 seconds.

Investigate
Find out how long it took Rankis to fall 10,000 feet before opening his chute.

AUGUST 5

1914

The first electric traffic lights are installed, in Cleveland Ohio.

Investigate
Brainstorm ways to control traffic without lights.

Mental Math: How old is the traffic light?

Estimate how long a nearby traffic light "stays green"; then check the actual time it does. Check out other events that seem to take a long time, then time them.

1989

At the Anglo-Chinese School in Singapore, 8,238 people play musical chairs.

Investigate
Invite the class to play musical chairs while someone keeps track of the time it takes to go from everybody's having a chair to just one person sitting. Then think about how long the game probably took when 8,238 people played it. How might the game be shortened?

AUGUST 6

1762

John Montagu, Fourth Earl of Sandwich, is born. According to the story that has, by now, assumed the status of myth, John Montagu later invents the sandwich when he doesn't want to take a break from playing cards to eat a proper meal, instead telling a servant to bring him some meat put between two pieces of bread.

Investigate

If you can use white or wheat bread, chunky or smooth peanut butter, and grape or raspberry jam, how many different variations of peanut butter and jelly sandwiches can you make? What if you also had rye bread and blackberry jam?

1926

Nineteen-year-old Gertrude Ederle becomes the first woman to swim the English Channel, completing the feat in 14 hours, 31 minutes. As of May 1995, 4,363 people have made 6,333 attempts to swim the Channel. Of these, 467 of them (310 men and 157 women) have made 732 successful crossings of the 35-mile distance. (Alison Streeter skewed the numbers by swimming the Channel a record 27 times.) The men's record is now 7 hours, 17 minutes; the women's record is 7 hours, 40 minutes.

Investigate

Mental Math: What year was Gertrude Ederle born?

How do these swimmers' times compare with those of people running the mile?

**1762
Fourth Earl of Sandwich**

AUGUST 7

1807

The *Clermont* steamboat, designed by Robert Fulton, makes its first trial trip—from New York City to Albany, a distance of 150 miles. It takes 32 hours. He repeats the trip ten days later, taking passengers.

Investigate
How many miles an hour does the boat average?

Estimate how long it would take a person to walk this same distance. How many footsteps would that be?

1958

The *Nautilus*, the world's first atomic submarine, completes its historic four-day undersea voyage across the top of the world (under the polar ice cap), traveling a distance of 1,830 miles. This establishes a new, shorter route to Europe from the Pacific. It also adds to our knowledge of the subsurface of the Arctic basin. The submarine has been converted into a museum
You can take a virtual tour online: *http://www.ussnautilus.org*. The site includes a *Nova* program.

Investigate
How many hours are there in four days? How many miles per hour did the submarine average?

AUGUST 8

1914

Antarctic explorer Ernest Shackleton sets sail from Plymouth, England, on the *Endurance*, a wooden ship built especially for Arctic rigors. The 300-ton ship is 144 feet long and built of wooden planks up to $2\frac{1}{2}$ feet thick. The ship has a crew of 28 men.

Competition to be part of this crew was fierce. One man chosen was Thomas McLeod, who brought 27 years of experience to this sailing, having run away to sea at age 14.

Investigate
How old was Thomas McLeod when he joined the crew?

1986

Four people begin a bicycle trip from Prudhoe Bay, Alaska. Their goal is to bike to the other end of the Americas. On June 13, 1987, they arrive at Beagle Channel, in Argentina.

Investigate
Get out the maps and figure the approximate distance they traveled.

How many days does the trip take?

AUGUST 9

1607

A Thanksgiving Day service is held on this day by colonists—in Phippsburg, Maine!

Investigate
Mental Math: How many years ago did this feast take place?

Since cornmeal was one of the most plentiful foods, alter a cornbread recipe so it makes enough for your class.

1829

The first U.S. locomotive makes its run on the tracks of the Delaware and Hudson Railroad between Carbondale and Honesdale, Pennsylvania. It is a seven-ton engine and travels at a speed of ten miles an hour.

1829
Pennysylvania

Investigate
How long would it take your parents to get to work if they traveled at ten miles per hour?

AUGUST 10

1874

Herbert Hoover, who will become the 31st President of the United States, is born. Orphaned at age eight, he was raised by relatives. Interested in mathematics, he studied engineering in college. He worked in mines in Australia and China. In addition to becoming President, he also wrote sixteen books, ranging from *Fishing for Fun* to the translation of a sixteenth-century book on mining called *De Re Metallica*.

Investigate
Did you ever think about how many words are in a book? Come up with a method for figuring out—without counting every word. Then, figure out about how many words Hoover wrote in his sixteen books (assume each book is 300 pages long).

Mental Math: How long ago was Herbert Hoover born? He was sworn in as President in March, 1929. How old was he then?

1986

A giant panda is born in China, an event hailed by everyone trying to preserve the species from extinction. The panda is a member of the raccoon family, and its natural habitat is the high mountain bamboo forests of central China.

Among many panda sites on the Web, these offer lots of facts and videos: *http://www.accessatatlanta.com/partners/zooatlanta/pandas* and *http://www.chinaunique.com/Panda/panda.htm*.

Investigate
Mental Math: How old is this panda today?

AUGUST 11

1909

The *Arapahoe* is the first American ship to send an SOS, the universal distress signal, as it flounders off the coast of Cape Hatteras, North Carolina.

Investigate
Invent a mathematical code that will enable you to communicate ten important messages quickly.

1929

A bus night coach, called an automobile bus, makes its first run between Los Angeles and San Francisco, California. The car is made of duralumin and provides seating and sleeping accommodation for 26 people. The bus has two lavatories, a kitchen, and a pantry, and it carries a crew of three: pilot, steward, and porter.

Investigate
Draw up plans for the interior of a vehicle like this. Start by finding out the dimensions of current buses.

How does the ratio of crew to passengers compare with that of today's passenger airplanes?

How does the ratio of lavatories to people compare with that at your school?

AUGUST 12

1925

Ross and Norris McWhirter are born. They later create *The Guinness Book of World Records* and become the first authors to sell more than 25 million copies of a single title.

Investigate
Share an "amazing number" anecdote from *The Guinness Book of World Records* with the class.

1980

Indah, an orangutan, is born at the National Zoo in Washington, D.C. She weighs just two pounds at birth and is placed in an incubator.

Investigate
Investigate birth weights of various creatures. Display your data graphically.

AUGUST 13

1889

William Gray, of Hartford, Connecticut, patents the first coin-operated telephone.

Investigate
What are the fewest coins you'd need, and the most possible coins you could use, to make calls costing $.35, $.45, $.85, and $.95?

1914

Carl Wickkman starts the Greyhound bus company, in Hibbing, Minnesota, the first bus line in the United States.

Investigate
Get a schedule from a national bus company and plan a cross-country trip by bus. Do you want to get there quickly or see interesting

sites along the way? How much will the trip cost in bus fare?

AUGUST 14

1873

The first issue of *Field and Stream* magazine is published.

Investigate
Find out what magazines arrive at your home. Bring the list to school. Compare with classmates and make a graph titled "Our Families' Magazines."

1912

Julia Child is born in Pasadena, California. She later writes many books about cooking and is the star of television shows about cooking. Her birthday is now celebrated as International Gourmet Day.

Investigate
Mental Math: How old is Julia Child today?

Discuss how math is important to cooking.

AUGUST 15

1848

M. Waldo Hancheett, of Syracuse, New York, receives patent number 5,711 for the dental chair. It has a headrest, and the positions of the seat and back are changeable.

Investigate
Mental Math: How long has the dental chair been around?

1914

The Panama Canal opens to commercial traffic. The *Ancon* is the first regular merchant vessel to traverse the canal from ocean to ocean, a distance of 50.72 miles. It takes

eight hours. Today the Panama Canal carries over fifteen thousand ships per year, earning more than 140 million dollars in tolls. Ship tolls are charged by the ton, with the average toll being about 10,000 dollars. In 1975, the *Queen Elizabeth* II pays the highest toll ever: $42,077.88. In 1928, Richard Halliburton swims the canal. His weight is 140 pounds, and his toll is 36 cents.

Investigate
Why is it worth it for a large ship to pay a $10,000 toll to go through the Panama Canal rather than just go around?

AUGUST 16

1948

Babe Ruth dies at age 53. The left-handed pitcher and "sultan of swat" hit 714 home runs in 22 major league seasons and played in 10 World Series. His body lies in state at the entrance of Yankee Stadium. Thousands of people wait in line for hours to walk by and pay their respects.

Investigate
Mental Math: What year was Babe Ruth born?

Choose another baseball player and compare his home run statistic with that of Babe Ruth.

1988

Chinese and Canadian scientists find fossils in Inner Mongolia of a group of baby ankylosaur dinosaurs that died 75 million years ago. These fossils are recent vintage compared to the *acasta gneisses*, a block of metamorphic rocks about 200 miles north of Yellowknife, Northwest Territories, Canada; these rocks are 4 billion years old. Information on rock and fossil sites in your area can be obtained by writing the United States Geological Survey, General Services

Building, 18th and F Streets, NW, Washington, DC 20242.

Investigate
Write both the fossil age and the rock age in scientific notation. For example, 6,000 is scientific notation is 6×10^3.

AUGUST 17

1807

Forty passengers, mostly friends and relatives, depart New York City for Albany, New York, aboard Robert Fulton's paddlewheel steamboat *The Steamboat* (later renamed the *Clermont*) on its 150-mile maiden voyage. Achieving an upstream speed of about five miles per hour, *The Steamboat* easily passes other ships on the river.

Investigate
How long did it take the steamboat to reach its destination?

1978

Carrying a crew of three, the *Double Eagle* II lands in Misserey, France, about 60 miles west of Paris, completing the first balloon crossing of the Atlantic, in 137 hours, 3 minutes. The balloon took off from Presque Isle, Maine.

Investigate
Calculate the distance of the trip. What was the balloon's average speed?

AUGUST 18

1888

Vincent van Gogh writes his friend and fellow artist Emile Bernard from Provence, in the south of France: "I am thinking of decorating my studio with half a dozen pictures of sunflowers, a decoration in which the raw or broken chrome yellows will blaze forth on various backgrounds."

Investigate
Use a picture of a sunflower (or, better, the real thing!) to explore Fibonacci numbers. The seedhead of a sunflower usually has 55 spirals going clockwise and 89 spirals going counterclockwise. Smaller sunflowers have 34 and 55 spirals. These are all Fibonacci numbers.

Generate Fibonacci numbers by starting with 1 + 1 and then getting the next number by adding together the two previous numbers.

1977

To celebrate the Cyclone's 50th birthday, Richard Rodriguez, a 19-year-old college student, rides this Coney Island roller coaster—for 103 hours 55 minutes! That's 2,361 straight rides. He sets a roller-coaster-riding record and inaugurates a new sport—roller coaster marathons. On July 12, 1988, the Cyclone joined the World Trade Center, the Statue of Liberty, and the Brooklyn Bridge as official historic sites.

American Coaster Enthusiasts can be found at *www.aceonline.org*. For photos of the Cyclone, go to *http://www.joyrides.com* and *http://www.astroland.com*.

Investigate
How many days did Rodriguez stay on the Cyclone?

How long did a single ride take?

AUGUST 19

1785

Seth Thomas, future clock manufacturer, is born.

Investigate
Come up with a list of things you can do in one minute, then have a friend time you while you test your list.

1856

Gail Borden, of Brooklyn, New York, receives patent number 15,553 for concentrated milk. Borden's first two business ventures fail. Finally, in 1861, he establishes a factory in Wassaic, New York. This became the Borden Company, which now has factories from coast to coast.

Investigate

How many gallons of milk does your class drink in a day? a week? the entire school year?

AUGUST 20

1811

Sixty-eight-year-old Thomas Jefferson writes to a friend, "No occupation is so delightful to me as the culture of the earth, and no culture is comparable to that of the garden. . . . But though an old man, I am but a young gardener." After leaving the White House and returning to Monticello, Jefferson plants 250 varieties of vegetables and 150 varieties of fruit trees. Peas are his favorite—he grows 22 varieties.

Investigate

Conduct a schoolwide survey: what are the favorite and most-hated vegetables?

Make a graph depicting the vegetables offered in the cafeteria over the period of a month.

1989

Antarctic explorer Will Steger notes that Victor Boyarsky, a scientist studying ozone and weather, is trying to thaw a tube of toothpaste by holding the end of it in his cup of hot water, a sure sign that the weather is colder than –40 degrees. Steger notes that it's also a sign that Victor is using Russian toothpaste. Colgate doesn't freeze until –60 degrees.

Investigate

With your parents' permission, design an experiment to test the freezing times of various foods.

AUGUST 21

1988

Antarctic explorer Will Steger notes that he and his fellow crew members spend about five hours ever day "unpacking and packing, setting up and tearing down camp." They spend about seven hours traveling. Caches of supplies have been laid out along their route. Each team member has a ration of 36 ounces of food per day, but they need to eat about 5,000 calories a day. Later in this expedition, Steger notes that after his 197th day of oatmeal and peanut butter for breakfast, he'd "kill for fruit."

Investigate

Plan daily menus that contain 5,000 calories but do not exceed 36 ounces.

1994

In Fort Collins, Colorado, Anni Kremi sets a record by throwing a flying disk 447 feet, 3 inches. The record for men is 656 feet, 2 inches, set by Scott Stokely in 1995.

Investigate

Along with your classmates, mark off 447 feet, 3 inches on the playground and then establish your own personal best Frisbee efforts within that distance.

AUGUST 22

1818

The *Savannah*, a 350-ton, fully rigged wooden steamboat, built at Corlear's Hook, New York, is launched. She has one engine of 90 horsepower, and on June 20, 1819, becomes the first steamboat built in

America to cross the Atlantic Ocean. Although she has 32 staterooms, no passengers are willing to make this initial 29-day Atlantic trip.

Investigate
Mental Math: What day did the *Savannah* set out on her Atlantic trip?

1989

Nolan Ryan strikes out his 5,000th batter, the first pitcher to do so.

Investigate
Research some of Ryan's other records.

Examine the number 5,000 and come up with creative ways to picture or explain it.

AUGUST 23

1993

At the Reptile House of the National Zoological Park in Washington, D.C., seventeen Komodo dragons emerge from twenty-four eggs that had been laid 216 days earlier at the Cincinnati Zoo. (The National Zoo's female dragon had been sent there on a breeding loan program.) The eggs were recovered from a nest the female had dug two feet underground and brought back to the National Zoo for incubation. Thirteen of the dragons survive. On October 1, two dragons stay in Washington and others find new homes at zoos in Atlanta, New Orleans, Honolulu, Albuquerque, Fort Worth, and St. Louis. This is the first successful breeding of Komodo dragons outside Indonesia, where Komodo dragons have been acknowledged as a national treasure since 1910. The number of Komodo dragons in the wild is estimated to be between 2,000 and 5,000. In captivity, there are 30 adult dragons in the world, so the survival of 13 dragons from the

24 eggs is named the "most significant animal husbandry event of the year." The adult Komodo dragon is 10 feet (3 meters) long.

Investigate
What day were the eggs laid?

Make a mural that depicts a 10-foot dragon lizard and shows the relative size of other animals.

1994

Fred Lebow, the creator of the New York City Marathon, is inducted into the National Track Hall of Fame. In November 1992, when his brain cancer was in remission, Lebow ran the marathon for the first time since 1976. He completed the 26-mile-385-yard course in 5 hours, 32 minutes, 34 seconds. Grete Witz, of Norway, nine-time women's winner, ran as his partner for the full distance.

In 1970, the first year of the New York City Marathon, 127 runners started and 55 finished. The runners kept circling Central Park for the distance. By 1989, there were 24,996 starters and 24,314 finishers, and they ran through all five boroughs of New York City.

Investigate
Which race had a higher percentage of finishers: 1970 or 1989? Explain your reasoning.

AUGUST 24

1869

Cornelius Swarthout, of Troy, New York, patents the waffle iron.

Investigate
Brainstorm a list of favorite things to put on waffles. Then choose any four and figure out how many waffles you'd need to layer these additions in all possible sequences.

1903

A horse named Lou Dillon establishes a record of 1 minute, $58\frac{1}{2}$ seconds for trotting one mile at Readville, Massachusetts.

Investigate
At this speed, how far would Lou Dillon trot in five minutes? half an hour?

AUGUST 25

1875

Captain Matthew Webb begins his swim from Dover, England. Twenty-one hours, forty-five minutes later, he completes his swim at Cap Gris-nez, France, and becomes the first person to swim across the English Channel. The distance is 56 kilometers (35 miles). The England-to-France crossing is considered more difficult than crossing from France to England.

Investigate
Check out some other swimming records. What conclusions can you make about the difficulty of this swim?

1916

The National Park Service is established under the Department of the Interior. The director receives 4,500 dollars a year.

Investigate
How much does the director make per hour if he works a fifty-hour week?

AUGUST 26

1768

Captain James Cook sets off for Tahiti on the *Endeavor*. The Royal Society has convinced the British government to fund an expedition to observe the transit of the planet Venus across the sun from the vantage point of the South Pacific and also to establish previously unknown longitudes. Captain Cook makes sure the *Endeavor* is stocked with enough food to feed 94 men for two years. This includes 34,000 pounds of bread.

Extensive Web sites are available, including *http://www.geocities.com/thetropics/7557* and *http://winthrop.webjump.com*.

Investigate
How much bread does Cook expect his crew to eat each day?

1981

Deep-sea divers find one of the two safes from the wreck of the *Andrea Doria*, off Nantucket, Massachusetts. People believe the liner, which sank in July of 1956, carried one million dollars in cash and jewels.

Investigate
Mental Math: How long was the *Andrea Doria* on the ocean floor before this safe was recovered?

AUGUST 27

1912

The first Tarzan story, by Edgar Lee Burroughs, appears in a magazine.

Investigate
Mental Math: How old is Tarzan?

1955

The Guinness Book of World Records is first published. Since then, over 70 million copies have been sold.

coldest
tallest
longest
most
shortest
biggest
slowest
fastest
highest

Investigate
How many copies of this book, on average, are sold each year?

AUGUST 28
1917

Ten suffragists are arrested as they picket outside the White House, demanding the right to vote. In October, four are sentenced to six months in prison. On November 10, forty-one more protesting women are arrested. The House of Representatives passed the woman suffrage amendment to the Constitution in May 1919; the Senate did so in June of that year. Tennessee was the thirty-sixth state to ratify the amendment, completing the approval by three quarters of the states necessary to made the amendment law. On August 26, 1920, the secretary of state signed the Proclamation of the Woman Suffrage Amendment, giving public notice that the nineteenth amendment was in effect. The first woman suffrage amendment was presented to Congress in 1868.

Investigate
Mental Math: Since the introduction of the Amendment in 1868, how long did it take women to get the right to vote? For how many years now have women had the right to vote?

1963

More than 200,000 people participate in a march on Washington, D.C., the largest civil rights demonstration to date. People march from the Washington Monument to the Lincoln Memorial. Martin Luther King, Jr., the last to speak, gives his "I have a dream" speech. This demonstration is credited with the passage of the Civil Rights Bill of 1964. "We Shall Overcome" was the theme song of this march.

Investigate
Come up with a method for figuring out how many people, standing close together, could fit in your classrooms. Then figure out how many classrooms it would take to hold 200,000 people.

AUGUST 29
1931

The longest dance marathon in U.S. history begins. It lasts 308,908 minutes.

Investigate
On what day did this marathon end?

1957

Senator Strom Thurmond of North Carolina sets a record in the U.S. Senate by speaking for twenty-four hours and eighteen minutes.

Investigate
Read aloud a page from a book and have a friend time how long it takes you. How many pages could you read in twenty-four hours and eighteen minutes?

1893

Esther Cleveland is born, the only child of a President to be born in the White House. Her parents, President Grover Cleveland and Frances Folsom, were married on June 2, 1886, in the Blue Room. So far, Cleveland is the only President to be married in the White House. President John Tyler had the largest family—fifteen children by two wives. After he was elected, all of Tyler's children came to the White House to live with him—even those who had left home and married.

Investigate
What is the average number of children in your class's households?

1916

Aboard the Chilian rescue ship *Yelcho*, Antarctic explorer Ernest Shackleton finally reaches the crew of his ship, which has been marooned on Elephant Island since January 18, 1915.

There are many Web sites honoring Shackleton and his crew, including *http:/www.pbs.org/wgbh/nova/shackleton*.

Investigate
How many days had the men been on Elephant Island?

AUGUST 31

1886

An earthquake with a magnitude of 7.6 hits Charleston, South Carolina, leveling most of

1987

FIRST PLACE

10th Annual New Jersey Championship Tomato Weigh-in

the city. This is the second-largest mid-plate earthquake recorded in North America. You can learn about earthquakes online at *http://www.civeng.carleton.ca/cgi-bin/quakes.*

Investigate
Review the Richter scale and powers of 10.

1987

George Bucsko wins the 10th annual New Jersey Championship Tomato Weigh-in with a jumbo 4.352-pound tomato. (It's amazing how much tomatoes "shrink" when they are cooked.)

Investigate
Along with each of your classmates, bring in a tomato. Weigh the tomatoes and analyze the results. What is their total weight? What is the weight range of the tomatoes brought in? the weight mode? the average weight?

S E P T E M B E R

SEPTEMBER 1

1916

A federal child labor act passes, regulating products made by children. (The federal government does not have the power to regulate state labor, so it regulates the products transported between states.) In 1918, the law was declared unconstitutional by the Supreme Court—the Court held the law was an invasion of states' rights. But states began passing their own laws to protect children.

Investigate
Take a poll of jobs kids have and jobs they'd like to have. Display the results in a graph.

1968

The first school for circus clowns is established, in Venice, Florida. Twenty years later, it had graduated more than 1,000 certified clowns. The college is tuition-free, not wanting to present financial barriers that might prevent clown hopefuls from realizing their dreams. Prospective students are asked a series of provocative questions:

◆ List five movies you'd like to see again.

◆ List five of your favorite books.

◆ Name your favorite foods.

◆ What part of the world would you most like to visit? Why?

◆ Describe your first proud accomplishment.

◆ What is the most important life lesson you've learned to date?

◆ When was the last time you cried? For what reason?

The college was closed in the late 1990s. A clown scorecard for rating clowns is available at *http://cheesecakeandfriends.com /c-scorsh.htm*.

Investigate
Along with your classmates, answer some or all of these questions; compile the resulting information into a class profile.

SEPTEMBER 2
490 B.C.

Phidippides runs the original marathon, 26 miles from Marathon to Sparta, to seek help in repelling the Persian army. Help being unforthcoming, he runs back to Marathon on September 4. The marathon is revived at the 1896 Olympic Games in Athens.

Investigate
How many years passed between the two marathons?

1893

Beatrix Potter writes what becomes one of the most famous letters in literature—a "picture letter" to five-year-old Noel, who is sick in bed: "My dear Noel, I don't know what to write to you, so I shall tell you a story about four little rabbits whose names were Flopsy, Mopsy, Cottontail, and Peter. . . . "

Investigate
How many other ways could Potter have ordered the names in introducing these four rabbits? How will you know you have come up with all possible combinations?

SEPTEMBER 3
1838

Dressed as a sailor, African American Frederick Augustus Washington Bailey boards a train in Baltimore, Maryland, a slave state, and rides to Wilmington, Delaware, where he boards a steamboat to the free city of Philadelphia. From there he takes the train to New York City and enters the underground railway system that guides runaway slaves to safety. Bailey, born in February 1817, changed his name to Douglass and became a noted journalist, orator, and antislavery leader.

Investigate
Mental Math: How old was Bailey/Douglass when he made his daring dash to freedom?

1985

The wreck of the *Titanic*, the luxury liner that sank in 1912 on its maiden voyage, is found 400 miles (640 kilometers) south of Newfoundland.

Visit the Titanic online at *http://titanic .eb.com* and *http://www.titanic-online.com*.

The wreck of the Titanic is found.

Investigate

Mental Math: How long had the *Titanic* been on the ocean floor before it was discovered? How old is it today?

SEPTEMBER 4

1848

Lewis Howard Lattimer, future inventor, is born. He works with Edison and supervises the installation of electric lighting in Philadelphia, London, and Montreal.

Investigate

Invite an electrician to talk to the class about the mathematics involved in electrical circuitry.

1882

The first electric station to supply light and power, the Edison Electric Illuminating Company in New York City, opens; it has a single engine that generates power for 800 lightbulbs. Within fourteen months, the company has 508 subscribers and is generating power for 12,732 lightbulbs.

Investigate

How many lightbulbs are in your house? How does this number compare with the number per subscriber in New York City in 1883?

SEPTEMBER 5

1776

Standardized naval uniforms are adopted. Captains wear a blue coat with red labels, a stand-up collar, yellow buttons, blue breeches, and a red waistcoat with yellow lace. Sailors have a green coat with white cuffs, and white waistcoats.

You can visit the Department of the Navy Historical Center online at *http://www.history.navy.mil/index.html*.

Investigate

How many different uniforms can you create by recombining the red and white waistcoats and the blue and green coats?

1834

The first village improvement society is founded, in Stockbridge, Massachusetts, "to improve and ornament the streets . . . and to do acts as shall tend to improve and beautify the village."

Investigate

Along with your classmates, come up with a plan for improving and beautifying your school. Include a proposed time frame showing how many people will work on each project and how long it will take.

SEPTEMBER 6

1578

Sir Francis Drake reaches the Pacific Ocean on one of the epic voyages of all time: he left Britain on December 13, 1577, and arrived home September 22, 1580.

Investigate

How many days was Drake at sea? What other facts can you find out about Drake's voyage?

1996

According to *The Guinness Book of World Records*, 1,665 people from the University of Guelph, Canada, maneuver together as the largest human centipede. To qualify, they had to walk 98.5 feet with their ankles tied together without anyone's falling down.

Investigate

Form teams and measure the distances each team can walk with their ankles tied together. Give each team three trials. Report the results.

SEPTEMBER 7

1975

Members of the Westside Assembly of God Church in Davenport, Iowa, make a 5,750-pound iced lollipop. The original Popsicle was invented in 1905 by 11-year-old Frank Epperson. He left a soft-drink mixture outside overnight with a stirring stick in it and found it frozen the next morning. Eighteen years later Frank developed a business producing Episicles in seven flavors. The name was later changed to Popsicle. Now, more than three million Popsicles, in 30 flavors, are sold a year. Orange is the most popular flavor.

Investigate

Mental Math: How old is Epperson when he starts producing his Episicles?

1996

The Regulars, a small group of bird-watchers in New York's Central Park, spot a

September 7, 1975

Connecticut warbler, one of the most elusive of birds.

Investigate

Set up a bird-watching station. Over one week, keep track of how many birds you spot each day. Can you identify the birds by type? Display the statistics in a graph.

SEPTEMBER 8

1866

James and Jennie Bushnell become the proud parents of sextuplets in Chicago, Illinois. Three boys and three girls are born. This is the first recorded live birth of sextuplets.

Investigate

If parents have one child, there are two equally likely possibilities, with a $\frac{1}{2}$ chance of having a girl and a $\frac{1}{2}$ chance of having a boy. When parents have twins, there are four equally likely possibilities: both are girls, both are boys, the firstborn is a girl and the second is a boy, or the firstborn is a boy and the second is a girl. Two of the four possibilities, or $\frac{1}{2}$, are having one of each—a girl and a boy. There is a $\frac{1}{4}$ chance that they'll have two girls and a $\frac{1}{4}$ chance they'll have two boys. Figure out what the possibilities are with triplets, quadruplets, quintuplets, and sextuplets.

1984

About 6,000 of the 7,000 students at Notre Dame University travel in what may have been the longest bus caravan ever. They go from South Bend to Indianapolis, Indiana in 147 buses, to see the sold-out Notre Dame-Purdue football game.

Investigate

How long would a caravan of 147 buses be? About how many students rode on each bus?

SEPTEMBER 9

1850

California enters the Union as the 31st state. The number 31 is an interesting number: it is the sum of five powers of 2 (1 + 2 + 4 + 8 + 16); there are 31 days in most months; there are 31 letters in Cyrillic (Russian) alphabet.

Investigate
Is 31 a prime number? What else can you discover about the number 31?

1998

Keiko, the killer whale who leaps to fame in the movie *Free Willy*, heads to a new life. Weighing in at 9,000 pounds, Keiko is hoisted from his tank at the Oregon Coast Aquarium in Newport, Oregon; he then rides on a flatbed truck to the airport, where an Air Force C-17 plane takes him on a 5,341-mile flight to the Westman Islands, Iceland. On board the plane with Keiki are the Air Force crew, four veterinarians, and five animal-care specialists. Keiki travels in a water-filled box and is rubbed with lanolin balm and ice to keep him cool. The temperature in the jet is kept at 50 degrees.

In Iceland, Keiko's floating sea pen is 250 feet long, 100 feet wide, and 27 feet deep. That's about 60 percent bigger than his pool in Oregon. The pen has nylon mesh rope sides, allowing ocean water and small fish to move freely.

Investigate
Estimate about how long Keiko's flight takes.

How much mesh rope did the pen builders need to order?

SEPTEMBER 10

1904

The *Discovery* steams into Portsmouth, England. An expedition under the leader-ship of Robert Falcon Scott has returned from an Antarctic voyage that began on July 31, 1901. On February 14, 1904, the ship broke free of the ice holding it captive at McMurdo Sound and began the voyage home. (You can visit Antarctica online at *http://www.theice.org*.)

Investigate
How many days had the *Discovery* and its crew been gone?

1913

The Lincoln Highway (Route 30) opens. It is the first coast-to-coast paved road, extending from New York to California.

Investigate
Which 13 states does this highway traverse?

What's the fewest number of states you have to drive through to travel from New York to California?

SEPTEMBER 11

1928

The Yelloway Bus Line begins coast-to-coast service from Los Angeles to New York City. Three 26-passenger buses leave daily from each terminal. They cover 3,433 miles in 5 days, 14 hours.

Investigate
Mental Math: How many people leave each day in each direction if every bus is full?

1993

The New York Guild of Chefs makes a rice pudding weighing 2,146.6 pounds.

Investigate
How many people do you think this rice pudding served? Devise a plan to figure it out.

SEPTEMBER 12

1984

Rhoshandiatellyneshiaunneveshenk Koyaanfsquatsiuty Williams is born in Beaumont, Texas. According to *The Guinness Book of World Records*, this is the longest name appearing on a birth certificate.

Investigate
Make a graph to show the lengths of the first names of the students in your class. Do the same for last names. Use the graphs to determine if, in your class, last names are typically longer, shorter, or the same length as first names.

1987

The original Winnie-the-Pooh, sixty-five years old, goes on display at the New York City Public Library.

Investigate
Mental Math: How old is Winnie-the-Pooh today?

Along with your classmates, celebrate Pooh by bringing stuffed bears to class. Measure their height and girth. Are all the bears' proportions similar?

SEPTEMBER 13

1857

Milton Snavely Hershey is born. Roald Dahl is born on this same date in 1916. Hershey and Dahl have something else important in common: chocolate! Hershey is the founder of the Hershey chocolate company. As a boy, Dahl is a chocolate taster for the Cadbury Chocolate Company. (The company sends samples of new candy bars to the boarding school Dahl attends. The students are asked to rate them.)

Investigate
Devise a ratings system for cafeteria food. Establish three or four criteria, then give a grade in a range (for example, from one to four). Every day, rate the food and tally the results. After you have kept track for a suitable period, write up your findings.

1965

New York Giant Willie Mays hits his 500th home run. On this same date in 1971, Baltimore Oriole Frank Robinson hits his 500th home run.

Investigate
Mental Math: How many years ago did Willie Mays hit his 500th home run? Frank Robinson?

SEPTEMBER 14

1814

Francis Scott Key, who has been aboard a ship in Baltimore harbor while the British bombard Fort McHenry, is inspired to write a song about the flag he sees flying this morning. "The Star-Spangled Banner" becomes the national anthem of the United States. The flag Scott sees was made by Mary Pickersgill, a widow raising a young child. She had been asked for "a large flag," and this one measures 42 feet by 30 feet.

Investigate
Do you think this flag was larger or smaller than the area of your classroom? Draw a 30-by-42-foot rectangle on the playground and find out.

1987

The most massive single issue of a newspaper is published, the Sunday *New York Times*; it weighs 12 pounds and contains 1,612 pages. According to *Audubon* magazine (March 1990), if you subscribe to a big-city newspaper, you will have to deal with 550 pounds of wastepaper each year. An average *New York Times* Sunday edition produces 8 million pounds of wastepaper.

Investigate
Weigh a week's worth of your local newspaper and then figure out how much wastepaper one subscription will generate in one year.

SEPTEMBER 15
1858

Overland mail service to the Pacific coast begins, using stagecoaches running between Tipton, Missouri, and San Francisco, California. The stagecoaches make trips twice a week, covering 2,800 miles in 25 days. The government signs a contract with the stage line, paying $600,000 a year to deliver the mail.

Investigate
How much is the stage company paid for each trip?

1982

USA *Today* begins publication. It is noted for keeping its stories short, using lots of color, and communicating information through graphs. It is also noted for providing helpful information about weather for business travelers. You can access USA *Today* weather online at *http://www.usatoday.com/weather /wfront.htm.*

Investigate
What is the difference in temperature between the hottest and coldest spots in the United States reported on the USA *Today* weather map?

What else can you find out from this map?

SEPTEMBER 16
1994

The town of Montebello, California, makes it into *The Guinness Book of World Records* by assembling a 3,960-pound burrito. Eggs, refried beans, cheese, tomatoes, lettuce, and salsa are wrapped in a 3,055.4-foot-long tortilla.

Investigate
How many people would you invite to a party at which you are serving a 3,055.4-foot-long burrito?

1995

In Bihar, India, Amresh Kumar Jha sets the record for balancing on one foot. He balances for 71 hours, 40 minutes.

Investigate
For how many days does Jha balance on one foot?

Can you balance longer on your left or right foot? Have a friend time you as you take three trials on each foot.

SEPTEMBER 17
1787

The Constitution is read aloud and approved, then signed by 39 of the remaining 42 delegates to the Continental Congress. Eighty-one-year-old Benjamin Franklin is too feeble to deliver his own speech, but his remarks are read by James Wilson. Franklin acknowledges that such a large group will reveal their prejudices and errors but that he is astonished "to find this system approaching so near to perfection as it does; and I think it will astonish our ene-

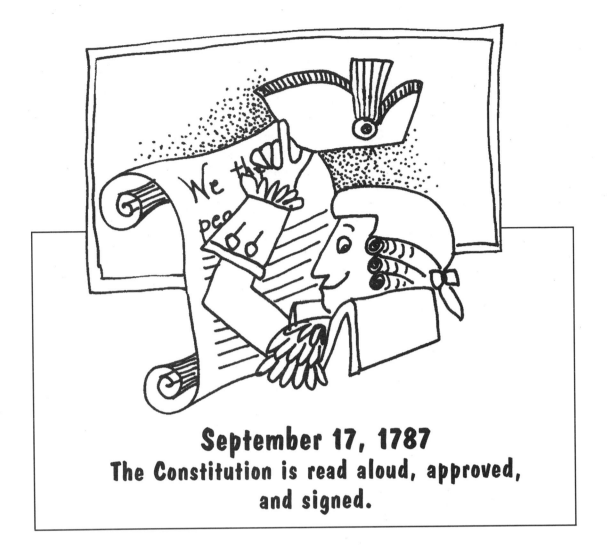

September 17, 1787
The Constitution is read aloud, approved, and signed.

mies, who are waiting with confidence to hear that our councils are confounded like those of the builders of Babel." We now celebrate September 17 as Citizenship Day.

Investigate
How old is our Constitution?

1989

On day 53 of the International Trans-Antarctica Expedition, Will Steger notes that the team has passed the 500-mile mark. "We've been on the ice more than fifty days already. . . . My mood isn't brightened when I pull out my *National Geographic* map of Antarctica and realize that in nearly two

months we've traveled about four inches. We still have two feet to go."

Investigate
What is the scale of the map Steger is looking at? How many miles did this expedition have left to go?

SEPTEMBER 18

1889

Jane Addams moves into Hull House, a dilapidated mansion on South Halsted Street in Chicago. Among Addams's many accomplishments are operating a cooperative boardinghouse for poor working women, lobbying for the passage of the first factory law in Illinois, offering shelter to homeless women, and organizing people to defeat corrupt politicians. She received the Nobel Peace Prize in 1931.

Investigate
Ask a local organizer of food kitchens or similar projects to visit your class and talk about the mathematics of keeping such endeavors going.

1983

British adventurer George Megan finishes a long walk. Starting six years earlier at the southern tip of South America, he finishes his trip in the Arctic—at Prudhoe Bay, Alaska.

Investigate
Consult maps and figure out how far George Megan walked.

SEPTEMBER 19
1970

The *Mary Tyler Moore Show* premiers, on CBS. It is unusual in that the central character is an independent career woman. The show ran new episodes for seven seasons, through September 3, 1977, with twenty-four episodes each season.

Investigate
How many original episodes were made in all?

Keep track of the TV you watch for a week. Make tally marks in one column when children are portrayed positively and in another column when they are portrayed negatively. Write up your conclusions, using the data you have compiled.

1992

Five women set a world record at the 64th Annual Idaho Spud Day celebration in

Shelley, Idaho, by peeling 1,064 pounds, 6 ounces of potatoes in 45 minutes. They don't waste the potatoes. When they are done peeling, they make everything from potato donuts to potato ice cream.

Investigate
Weigh two potatoes and then time yourself while peeling them. How do you compare with the ladies in Idaho?

SEPTEMBER 20
1984

Aarthur the aardvark is born at the Philadelphia zoo. Her name is later changed to Aava. An aardvark would make a good subject for a *cinquain*, a mathematical poem with the following characteristics:

Syllables	Description	Example
2	title	llama
4	description of title	camel cousin
6	action	climbs the Andes mountains
8	feeling	makes me glad to see her warm face
2	synonym for title	warm beast

Investigate
Create a cinquain about an aardvark.

1998

Baltimore Oriole Cal Ripken chooses to sit out the game, ending his streak of playing every game at 2,632 games, which is 502 more than Lou Gehrig's consecutive game streak. Ripken's streak begins on May 29, 1982.

Currently, the player with the most consecutive games is Albert Belle of the Chicago White Sox, with 325 games.

Investigate
Figure out in what year Albert Belle could break Ripken's record (2012). Remember, you must count the days in a baseball season, not in a year.

SEPTEMBER 21

1883

Cornell University, in Ithaca, New York, offers the first electrical engineering course.

Investigate
Ask an electrical engineer to talk to your class about electrical engineering courses today and about how mathematics applies to his or her job.

1994

Aleksandr Bendikov, of Mogilev, Belarus, stacks 522 dominoes on just one supporting domino.

Investigate
About how tall do you think the stack was?

Identify characteristics of the number 522.

SEPTEMBER 22

1941

The *Patrick Henry*, the first liberty ship in World War II, is launched. The ship has an overall length of 441 feet, a displacement of 14,000 tons, and a general cargo capacity of 9,146 tons. She (ships may have male names but they are still referred to as

"she") is built in 244 days. By 1943, ship builders worked around the clock and the time it took to build a liberty ship fell to 30 days.

Investigate
When did construction on the *Patrick Henry* begin?

1955

Commercial television was beamed into homes in Great Britain. Only six minutes of ads were allowed each hour and there was no Sunday morning TV permitted.

Investigate
How many minutes of ads are typically shown during an hour-long television show today? Watch an hour-long show and use a watch or timer to keep track. Compare your results with those of your classmates. What's the typical amount of time spent on ads during an hour of television?

SEPTEMBER 23

1806

After 2 years, 4 months, 10 days, the Lewis and Clark Expedition completes its exploration of the West and arrives back in St. Louis, Missouri.

Investigate
Mental Math: How many days did the expedition last?

1988

A male leatherback turtle is found on the beach at Harlech, Wales. It measures 9 feet, $5\frac{1}{2}$ inches from nose to tail and 9 feet across the front flippers. It weighs 2,120 pounds. The largest turtle found in the United

Harlech, Wales
September 23, 1988
A leatherback turtle weighs 2,120 pounds.

States, off Monterey, California, on August 29, 1961, measures 8 feet, 4 inches and weighs 1,908 pounds.

Investigate
About how many kids does it take to equal the Harlech turtle's weight? Estimate and then calculate.

SEPTEMBER 24
1988

Carl Lewis becomes the fastest human, clocking 9.92 seconds in the final race of the 100-meter dash at the Olympics in Seoul, South Korea. The next day, Florence Griffith Joyner becomes the fastest woman on earth, running the same distance in 10.54 seconds.

Investigate
Measure how far you can run in ten seconds. Do several trials and record your best time. Make a graph to show the results of the students in your class.

SEPTEMBER 25
1912

The Ford Motor Company establishes an eight-hour workday and a five-day week.

Investigate
This workday is still considered standard. Calculate the typical number of hours a person works a year.

Consider your own workday. How many hours a week are you in school? How many hours a year?

SEPTEMBER 26

1812

Davy Crockett enlists as a soldier in the War of 1812. He serves for three months and receives a stipend of $8.00 per month. He also receives an allowance of $38.80 for the care and feeding of his horse. In 1836, Crockett was the most famous defender of the Alamo against the attacking Mexican cavalry, led by Santa Ana.

Investigate
How much money did Crockett receive all together for his service in 1812?

1855

After searching for a job six days a week for six weeks, sixteen-year-old John D. Rockefeller is hired as an assistant book-keeper in Cleveland, Ohio. He works for three months as an unpaid apprentice and then receives retroactive pay of $50 for the three months. Later in life, history's first billionaire reflected, "As I began my life as a bookkeeper, I learned to have great respect for figures and facts, no matter how small they were. . . . I had a passion for detail."

Investigate
Assuming he worked five days a week, how much was Rockefeller paid each day for his first three months at that job?

How does Rockefeller's earnings compare with what a minimum-wage earner would receive for three months of work today?

1981

Aicama Zorba of La-Susa, an Old English mastiff who lives in Great Britain, dies. She is listed in *The Guinness Book of World Records* as "the heaviest and longest dog ever recorded." She weighed 343 pounds, stood 37 inches at the shoulder, and measured 8 feet, 3 inches from nose to tail.

Investigate
How do your pets and of those your class-mates measure up? Bring in weights and measurements and then figure out class averages.

SEPTEMBER 27

1998

The Yankees end the baseball season with more wins than any team, 116. The Florida Marlins have the worst record: 54 wins, 108 losses.

Investigate
How many games did the Yankees lose?

SEPTEMBER 28

551 B.C.

Confucius, future Chinese philosopher and teacher, is born. Confucius is the Latin trans-lation of his Chinese name, Kung-Fu-Tzu. This day is celebrated as Teachers' Day in Taiwan.

Investigate
Mental Math: How many years ago was Kung-Fu-Tzu born?

1698

Pierre de Maupertuis is born in Saint Malo, France. He was a member of an expedition to Laplane in 1736, which set out to measure the length of a degree along the meridian. His measurements verified Newton's predictions about the shape of the Earth. This measurement made de Maupertuis famous.

Investigate

Look up the longitude and latitude of your town. Then look up those of three other cities you'd like to visit. Do you notice anything about the numbers?

SEPTEMBER 29

1829

The Greater London Metropolitan Police—better known as Scotland Yard—is established by an act of Parliament. Scotland Yard is the site of the first headquarters.

Investigate

Mental Math: How old is Scotland Yard?

1992

At Fossil Rim Wildlife Center, in Glen Rose, Texas, Rachel, a six-year-old cheetah, gives birth to four healthy cubs. The cheetah is the fastest of all land animals, able to run up to 62 miles per hour (103 kilometers per hour) over short distances.

Investigate

Assuming that two of Rachel's cubs are female, chart three generations of cubs, assuming each time that half the offspring are female. (Remember that reproduction of wild animals held in captivity does not work mathematically; many other factors are involved!)

1841
Poughkeepsie, New York

SEPTEMBER 30

1841

Samuel Slocum, of Poughkeepsie, New York, patents the stapler, but he doesn't call it that. He calls it a "machine for sticking pins into paper."

Investigate

Mental Math: How old is the stapler?

1882

The first hydroelectric power plant is opened, in Appleton, Wisconsin. It has a dynamo of 180 lights, each with a candlepower of 10.

Investigate

Mental Math: Figure out the total candlepower.

OCTOBER

OCTOBER 1

1890

The Weather Service, which up to now has been part of the Army Signal Corps, has its name changed to the Weather Bureau by Congress and is transferred to the Department of Commerce. In 1965 it was made part of the Environmental Science Services Administration, and in 1970 it was made part of the National Oceanic and Atmospheric Administration and renamed the National Weather Service. You can check out weather online at *http://www.WHNT19 .com/kidwx/* and *http://www.usatoday.com /weather/wfront.htm.*

Investigate

Along with your classmates, identify cities anywhere in the world whose weather might be interesting to monitor. Put all the names in a box. Form teams and have each team pick a city from the box and track that city's weather for one month. Then find a way to display this information.

1971

Ten thousand visitors are ready when the gates of the Magic Kingdom at Walt Disney World open for the first time, in Orlando, Florida. There are seven different "lands" inside the Florida park, all based on favorite Disney themes. Disney World covers 30,000 acres; 12,000 acres have not yet been built on.

Investigate

If you have just one day to visit Disney World and can visit two of its "lands," how many different combinations do you have to choose from? How do you know you've considered them all?

OCTOBER 2

1872

Phileas Fogg, a character in Jules Verne's *Around the World in Eighty Days*, starts out to fulfill his famous bet—of twenty thousand pounds—that he can travel around the world in eighty days.

Investigate
Mental Math: By which day must Fogg complete his travels to collect on the bet?

1920

The only triple-header in baseball history is played, and the Cincinnati Reds win two out of three games from the Pittsburgh Pirates.

Investigate
What are the possible outcomes for a triple-header? For example, the Cincinnati Reds could win the first two and lose the third or the Pittsburgh Pirates could win the first and lose the next two, and so on.

OCTOBER 3

1906

One of the nation's pioneer retailers, W. T. Grant, opens a 25-cent department store on this day.

Investigate
How many different ways can you make 25 cents using different combinations of pennies, nickels, and dimes?

1922

Mrs. W. H. Felton, 87, of Georgia, is appointed to fill a vacant United States Senate seat, becoming the first woman senator.

Investigate
What percentage of U.S. Senators today are women? How many would there be if members of Congress represented the number of citizens?

OCTOBER 4

1777

General George Washington's force of 11,000 Continental Army soldiers and militiamen, divided into four columns, attack the British garrison at Germantown, Pennsylvania, just north of Philadelphia.

Investigate
How many members of the Continental Army are in each column?

1957

The first earth satellite is launched into space this day by the Soviet Union. The craft circles the earth every 95 minutes at almost 2,000 miles per hour. "Sputnik I" fell from the sky on January 4, 1958.

Investigate
How many times did the satellite circle the earth before falling from the sky?

OCTOBER 5

1952

After an 11-year run on ABC radio, "Inner Sanctum," a legendary weekly mystery series, is heard for the final time.

Investigate
How many times was "Inner Sanctum" heard on the radio?

1974

David Kunst arrives home in Waseca, Minnesota, completing the first verified walk around the world. He started on June 10, 1970, and has worn out 21 pairs of shoes.

Investigate
Estimate how many miles Kunst traveled and then figure out how many miles he got out of each pair of shoes.

OCTOBER 6
1857

The first notable chess tournament in the United States to achieve world standing is held by the American Chess Congress in New York City. Paul Morphy, a twenty-year-old chess wizard from New Orleans, wins first prize: a silver tray with an accompanying silver pitcher and four silver goblets. Chess, one of the oldest and most popular board games today, first appeared in sixth-century India.

Investigate
Why do or don't you think the game of chess is related to math?

1927

The first "talking" movie, *The Jazz Singer*, premiers. When Al Jolson sings "Toot, Toot, Tootsie, Goodbye," audiences in theatres stand up and cheer.

Investigate
Mental Math: How long have the "talkies" been around?

OCTOBER 7
1954

A giraffe named Carol arrives at a zoo in Miami. She has come by truck from New York because she is too tall for an airplane.

Investigate
About how many times taller is a grown giraffe than a grown man?

1954
Miami, Florida

How much does a giraffe's height grow from infancy to adulthood? How does this compare with the changes in height of humans?

1973

Instead of using their professional football tickets, 40,000 football fans watch games on TV.

Investigate
Research how many people are estimated to watch football on TV today on Monday nights. How does this number compare with the 1973 statistic?

OCTOBER 8
1956

Using just ninety-seven pitches against the Brooklyn Dodgers, twenty-seven-year-old New York Yankee Don Larsen hurls the only perfect game—no hits, no walks—in World Series history. By the ninth inning, with two out and a pinch hitter at the plate, Larsen recalls, "I was so weak in the knees . . . I thought I was going to faint. . . . I was so nervous with only one batter to go that I almost fell down. My legs were rubbery and my fingers didn't feel like they were on my hand. I said to myself, 'Please help me, somebody.'"

With the count one ball and two strikes, Larsen says he has no memory of the last pitch, but the umpire calls a strike and there's pandemonium in Yankee Stadium.

Investigate
If every batter went to a 3 and 2 count (with no foul balls), how many pitches would be thrown in a perfect game?

1944

Ozzie and Harriet Nelson make their CBS radio debut in *The Adventures of Ozzie and Harriet*. On February 20, 1949, their sons David, 12, and Ricky, 8, appear as themselves. The show premiers on television on October 3, 1952, and plays until the end of the 1965–66 season.

Investigate
How old is Ricky Nelson when the show is canceled?

OCTOBER 9
1915

The International Association for Criminal Identification is formed, in Oakland, California. It is the first international fingerprint society. On May 21, 1934, the citizens of Oskaloosa, Iowa, acting on a recommendation of the police chief, had themselves fingerprinted. Today, the FBI receives more than 34,000 sets of fingerprints every day.

Investigate
If all the fingers on one hand are printed, how many prints does the FBI analyze each day?

1997

Residents in and around El Paso, Texas, get to see something that happens about once a year somewhere in the world: a daytime meteor. Zooming along at 30,000 miles per hour, 10 to 15 miles above Earth, the meteor leaves behind a trail of white smoke that remains visible for ten minutes.

Investigate
Collect more statistics about meteors.

OCTOBER 10
1492

Columbus promises his desperate crew, whose threats of mutiny are growing louder, that if they don't spot land in three days he will turn back. Crew members don't know he has been fudging the logs, making things seem more hopeful than they are. When Columbus set out from Spain on August 3, there were 52 men aboard his flagship the *Santa Maria*, 18 men aboard the *Nina*, and another 18 men aboard the *Pinta*.

Investigate
How many men were making this trip and how many days had they been at sea on October 10?

1913

President Woodrow Wilson pushes a button, and more than 4,000 miles (6,437 kilometers) away in Panama, dynamite blasts away the last remaining piece of rock between the Atlantic and Pacific Oceans. The 50.72-mile (81.63-kilometer) project had been in progress since 1907. When it was finished, it had cost more than $365 million.

Investigate
How much did it cost per mile (or kilometer) to build the Panama Canal?

OCTOBER 11
1887

The "Comptometer," an adding machine invented by Doerr Eugene Felt (born March

18, 1862), of Chicago, Illinois, receives a patent. For more information, check *http://members.cruzio.com/~vagabond.*

Investigate

Mental Math: How old was Felt when he received the patent?

1963

A newspaper reports that women outnumber men by almost 4 million in the U.S.

Investigate

Research today's population and compare the statistics.

OCTOBER 12

1892

The Pledge of Allegiance is first recited in schools, in commemoration of the 400th anniversary of Columbus's voyage. The pledge had been published in *The Youth's Companion* a month earlier.

Investigate

Mental Math: How long ago was the Pledge of Allegiance published?

1920

Construction of the Holland Tunnel begins to provide a direct link between New Jersey and New York City. The tunnel has two tubes more than 8,000 feet (2,400 meters) long. It opens to traffic on November 13, 1927.

Investigate

How many days elapsed from the time construction began to when the Holland Tunnel opens?

At a speed of 45 mph, how long would it take to drive through the tunnel?

OCTOBER 13

1792

The cornerstone is laid for the building that is first called the President's Palace. Later, it becomes known as the White House. Today, it has 132 rooms and 160 windows, each 14 feet high and 5 feet wide. Blueprints of the White House are available from the National Park Service, White House Liaison, 1100 Ohio Drive SW, Washington, D.C. 20242. Virtual tours are available at *http://www.whitehouse.gov.*

Investigate

How many rooms does your school have? How many windows? Is the proportion of windows to rooms about the same as that of the White House?

1995

On Martha's Vineyard, the Massachusetts Striped Bass and Bluefish Derby ends at midnight, one month after it starts. Twelve-year-old, 85-pound Whitney Branch catches a 28.35-pound striped bass. Derby

1995
Martha's Vineyard, Massachusetts

participants contributed 5,000 pounds of fish fillets to the elderly.

Investigate
Approximately how many fish do the donated fillets represent?

OCTOBER 14

1993

The Food Bank for Monterey County, in Salinas, California, makes a lasagna weighing 8,188 pounds, 8 ounces and measuring 70 feet by 7 feet.

Investigate
How much lasagna, in pounds and size, do you think your class could eat?

1994

Fyona Campbell returns to John o'Groat's, Scotland, having walked 19,586 miles around the world since she left on August 16, 1983.

Investigate
Map out a route in the United States you could walk to equal Fyona's record.

OCTOBER 15

1892

The U.S. government convinces the Crow Indians to sell 1.8 million acres of their reservation for 50 cents per acre. On this day, by presidential proclamation, the land in the mountainous area of western Montana is opened to settlers.

Investigate
How much did the U.S. government pay for the reservation?

How much would this land cost today?

1997

At Black Rock Desert, in Nevada, a British jet-powered car named Thrust, driven by Andy Green, sets the first supersonic world speed record on land, clocking an average speed of 763.035 miles an hour. The car, weighing ten tons and having the horsepower of 1,000 Ford Escorts, contains two Rolls-Royce engines from a Phantom fighter jet and races on a 13-mile course.

Investigate
How long did it take the car to circle the 13-mile track once?

OCTOBER 16

1701

Yale University is founded, in Killingworth, Connecticut. In 1745, the school is moved to New Haven.

Investigate
Mental Math: How old is Yale? How long has it been in New Haven?

1758

Noah Webster, future teacher, journalist, and dictionary maker, is born.
   His birthday is now celebrated as Dictionary Day.

Investigate
In teams, think of ten words that would be important in a mathematics dictionary. Share your definitions with the class.

OCTOBER 17

1888

The keel of the U.S.S. *Maine* battleship is laid at the Brooklyn Navy Yard. She is 318 feet long, her draft is 21 feet, and she displaces 6,682 tons. All her engines combined total a horsepower of 9,000.

Investigate

Estimate a distance of 318 feet, then measure and find out how accurate you were.

1967

The *New York Times* Sunday edition has 15 sections, 946 pages, and weighs $7\frac{1}{2}$ pounds.

Investigate

Compare this edition of the *Times* with your local Sunday paper. Figure out how many times more sections, pages, and pounds there are in this particular *Times* than in your local Sunday paper.

OCTOBER 18

1989

In what is known as "the year of hope for elephants," the Convention on International Trade in Endangered Species (CITES) votes to ban the import/export of ivory or other elephant products. Before this ban, ivory sells at $200 a pound in Japan. Ivory comes from the elephants' second incisors, teeth that grow about 7 inches (18 centimeters) per year and can reach a length of 13 feet and weigh 200 pounds.

Investigate

Estimate the length of your own front teeth. What fraction are they of an elephant's tooth?

1995

In New York City, employees of Kentucky Fried Chicken make a chicken pie weighing 22,178 pounds and measuring 12 feet in diameter. In 1991 the citizens of Circleville, Ohio, to celebrate the town's 85th annual pumpkin show, made a pumpkin pie that weighed 300 pounds and measured 5 feet in diameter.

Investigate

Compare the diameter and weight of the chicken pie with those of the pumpkin pie. What does this tell you about the relationship between diameter and weight?

OCTOBER 19

1850

Annie Smith Peck is born. A world-renowned mountain climber, Peck climbed the Matterhorn in the Swiss Alps and the Peruvian peak Huascarian. In 1911, she climbed Mt. Coropuna, also in Peru, putting a "Votes for Women" banner at the top.

Investigate

Mental Math: How old was Annie Smith Peck when she climbed Mt. Coropuna?

1995

USA *Today* publishes a poll on the activities teenagers enjoy most. Tied for first place are spending time with friends and watching TV. The third most popular activity is listening to recorded music.

OCTOBER 20

1865

Philadelphia defeats Danville in baseball,
160 to 11.

Investigate
Mental Math: How many more runs did
Philadelphia score than Danville? What per-
cent of the total runs did Danville Score?

1984

The International Bureau of Weights and
Measures changes the official definitions of
metric measurements. The meter is rede-
fined as the distance traveled by light in a
vacuum in 1/299,792,458 second. Originally,
the meter was based on a geographical
measure, 1/10,000,000 of a quadrant of a
great circle on Earth.

Investigate
Acquire some experience with the metric
system by measuring your desk, the room,
yourself.

OCTOBER 21

1797

The U.S.S. *Constitution* sails from the Boston
Navy Yard. Paul Revere fashioned the spikes
and bolts that fasten the ship's timbers. She
carries 56 guns, and it takes 180 men to lift
the huge main anchors. Made from white
oak and yellow pine, the ship earned the
nickname "Old Ironsides" during the War of
1812 (British cannonballs bounced off her).
The ship was named a national shrine in
1940 and can be visited in the Boston Naval
Shipyard or online at *http://www
.ussconstitution.navy.mil.*

Investigate
Mental Math: How old was "Old Ironsides"
when she became a national shrine?

1879

After thirteen months of night-and-day
experimenting, Thomas Alva Edison produces the first electric incandescent lamp of
practical value. Edison applies for a patent
on November 4, 1879, which is granted
January 27, 1880. He holds the first public
demonstration on December 31, 1879. The
Pennsylvania Railroad Company runs special trains to Menlo Park, New Jersey, so an
eager public can attend.

Investigate
How many days after applying did it take for
the patent to be granted?

OCTOBER 22

1837

At age 20, Henry David Thoreau begins the
journal he will keep for the next 25 years.
More than two million words fill the 14 published volumes. Earlier, Thoreau has made a
few attempts to keep a journal, but when
Ralph Waldo Emerson asks him, "Do you
keep a journal?" he starts in earnest—and
sticks with it.

Investigate
About how many words did Thoreau write in
his journal each year?

Write a journal entry. If you write this same
number of words each day, how many words
will you have produced in one year?

1934

The first streamlined Pullman train leaves
Los Angeles at 10 P.M. It pulled into Grand
Central Terminal in New York City at 9:55
A.M. on October 25th, after having traveled

2,298 miles at an average speed of almost 60 miles per hour. The train is operated by a 900-horsepower V-type two-cylinder Diesel engine. It has a mail-baggage car, three sleeping cars, and a dining car.

Investigate
How many hours did the trip take?

OCTOBER 23

1752

French chef Nicolas Appert, future inventor of the bouillon cube and "father of canning," is born. In 1809 he invented a process to preserve food by heating and sealing it in airtight containers.

Investigate
Find out how many cans of food per student are in the homes of your classmates and graph your results.

1977

Wesley Paul, eight years old, of Columbia, Missouri, runs the New York City Marathon in 3 hours, 31 seconds.

Investigate
Mental Math: How old is Wesley Paul today?

OCTOBER 24

1836

Alonzo D. Phillips of Springfield, Massachusetts, receives a patent for the phosphorous friction safety match. Remember, it's important to "close cover before striking."

Investigate
Mental Math: How long ago was the match invented?

1891

William Martin is the winner of a bicycle race that began on October 18; the length of the race was 1,466.4 miles. (Ten laps on the circular track on which the race takes place equal one mile.) Forty bicyclists started the race; only six finish. William's prize is $2,000.

Investigate
Come up with some interesting math problems based on these numbers.

OCTOBER 25

1955

The microwave oven is introduced in Mansfield, Ohio, at the corporate headquarters of the Tappan Company with a price tag of $1,200. Tappan Company claims that it can cook eggs in 22 seconds and bacon in 90 seconds.

Investigate
Mental Math: How long ago was the microwave oven introduced?

Poll your classmates to see how many have a microwave oven at home. Display the results in a graph.

How much longer does it take to bake a potato in a conventional oven than in a microwave oven? Compare other cooking times.

1972

The first women to become FBI agents complete their training at the agency's facility in Quantico, Virginia. Susan Lynn Roley and Joanne E. Pierce graduate along with 45 men.

Investigate
What percentage of this class is women?

What percentage of your class is female?

OCTOBER 26

1861

Telegraph service becomes available from San Francisco to New York. It costs six dollars for every ten words.

Investigate
Examine a letter to the editor in your local paper. At six dollars for every ten words, how much would it have cost to send this letter by telegram from San Francisco to New York in 1861?

1958

The first New York–Paris transatlantic jet passenger service is inaugurated by Pan Am. The same day, the first New York–London transatlantic jet passenger service is inaugurated by BOAC.

Investigate
Mental Math: How many years have people been able to fly from New York to Paris and London?

OCTOBER 27

1858

Theodore Roosevelt is born. He later becomes the 26th U.S. President when William McKinley dies, on Sept. 14, 1901.

Investigate
Mental Math: How old was Theodore Roosevelt when he became President?

1904

The New York subway system opens. Each subway car, lit by 26 bulbs, has 52 seats. With Mayor George McClellan at the controls, a special four-car train full of guests travels more than nine miles around the city. The mayor is supposed to give the con-trols to a regular motorman once the train gets underway, but he enjoys himself so much he refuses to step aside. The train travels at speeds up to 40 miles per hour. The subway is so popular that by 1908 it averages 800,000 passengers a day. (Today, $3\frac{1}{2}$ million people ride the New York subway system every day.)

There is a great deal of subway information online, including *http://www.pbs.org/wgbh /amex/technology/nyunderground*.

Investigate
How many people took that inaugural trip?

OCTOBER 28

1886

The Statue of Liberty is dedicated in New York Harbor. Designed by the French sculptor Frederic Auguste Bartholdi, the statue is a gift from the people of France in commemoration of the hundredth anniversary of American independence. The right hand and torch had been part of Philadelphia's Centennial Exhibition in 1876. The statue is 151 feet high, not including the arm and the torch, and stands on a granite pedestal that is 155 feet high. The statue's arm, from shoulder to torch, measures 75 feet.

For a virtual tour, go to *http://www .nyctourist.com/liberty1.htm*.

Investigate
Mental Math: What is the distance from the base of the pedestal to the tip of the torch?

How does the length of the statue's arm compare with her height? How does the length of your arm compare with your height? Are the two proportions similar?

1965

The stainless steel arch Gateway to the West is completed, in St. Louis. Designed

10,540

1994
Keene, New Hampshire

by Finnish-American architect Eero Saarinen, the 630-foot-high parabolic arch, which also spans 630 feet, commemorates the city's role in the westward expansion of our nation after the Louisiana Purchase of 1803.

Investigate
Draw an arch that's as long as it is high.

OCTOBER 29

1945

The first commercially made ballpoint pens go on sale in New York City. The pens sell for $12.50.

Investigate
Mental Math: How long ago were the first commercially made ballpoint pens sold?

How does the 1945 price compare with a typical price today?

1994

People in Keene, New Hampshire, carve 10,540 jack-o'-lanterns for the city's Harvest Festival.

Investigate
Along with each of your classmates, bring a pumpkin to class. Estimate the length of string or yarn you will need to encircle your pumpkin. Compare weight-circumference ratios for all the pumpkins and look for patterns.

OCTOBER 30

1984

The 1984 Christmas stamp is issued. It is designed by Danny LaBoccetta, a fourth grader in Jamaica, New York.

Investigate
Mental Math: How old is Danny today?

1989

A rare African goliath frog captured on the Sanaga River, Cameroon, weighs 8 pounds, 1 ounce. With its legs extended, its length is $34\frac{1}{2}$ inches.

Investigate
Compare your own height with that of this frog. Stretched out, where would this frog come to on your body?

ME RARE!

1989
Sanaga River, Cameroon, Africa

OCTOBER 31

1906

British designer John Stuart Blackton produces the first animated cartoon, *Humorous Phases of Funny Faces*. The film uses stop-frame photography. In the film a man blows cigar smoke on a woman, and she disappears.

Investigate
Create a "flip-book" cartoon. How many "frames" do you think you'll need to convey a story? Before you begin, make a template for each frame by dividing an $8\frac{1}{2}$-by-11-inch sheet of paper into 12 equal squares; each square on this paper becomes one frame. (*Copier Creations*, by Paul Fleischman [HarperCollins, 1993], provides detailed guidance for this project.)

1941

Drilling is completed on the four granite presidential faces on Mount Rushmore, in South Dakota. The gigantic faces of Presidents George Washington, Thomas Jefferson, Abraham Lincoln, and Theodore Roosevelt are sixty feet high. Gutzon Borglum, the man who carves these heads out of the mountain, works with models on a scale of one to twelve: one inch on a model is one foot on the mountain.

Investigate
Make a scale drawing of your desk.

NOVEMBER

1800

John and Abigail Adams move into the White House, the first residents of the stately home in Washington, D.C. The house is not yet finished, and Mrs. Adams uses the East Room to dry the family laundry. At 79 feet, $\frac{1}{2}$ inch by 36 feet, 9 inches, the East Room is the largest room in the White House. It has been used as everything from a roller skating rink for Theodore Roosevelt's children to a wedding site for Lynda Bird Johnson to a performance arena for Whitney Houston.

You can visit the East Room online at *http://www.whitehouse.gov.*

Investigate

How many chairs could you set around the perimeter of the East Room?

1952

MAD magazine goes on sale. The motto of its mascot, Alfred E. Newman, is: "What, me worry?" Nationally, here are kids' top worries: fear of death of a family member, fear of embarrassment In school, fear of failing, and fear of not having friends. Typically, the majority of things that worry the majority of children are school related. According to national surveys, more than 50 percent of children think school, family, and the media ignore their feelings.

Investigate

Along with each of your classmates, write down the thing about which you worry the most. Drop the paper, unsigned, into a box. As a class, combine and classify all this information, and represent it on a graph.

NOVEMBER 2

1918

Approaching a subway station at 30 miles per hour—five times faster than it should have been going—the Brighton Beach express jumps the tracks, injuring 200 people, some of them fatally.

Investigate

How fast should the subway have been traveling?

1986

Grete Waitz and Bob Wieland both participate in the seventeenth annual New York City Marathon. Waitz finishes first for the women for the eighth time, with a time of 2 hours, 28 minutes, 6 seconds. Wieland is considered a winner too, even though it takes him 98 hours to finish. Wieland, who lost his legs in the Vietnam War, pulls himself along the route with his arms.

Investigate

How many days did it take Bob Wieland to finish the course?

NOVEMBER 3

1948

In one of the most famous newspaper headlines ever printed, the *Chicago Daily Tribune* proclaims, "Dewey Defeats Truman." The *Tribune*'s editors based the headline on the polls, which showed Dewey winning by a landslide. The publisher wanted to get a jump on the competition, so the paper was printed before the votes were counted.

Investigate

Try a "sampling" technique: poll a fraction of the class and make a prediction about the results of the entire class. Then poll the remainder of the class and evaluate your prediction.

1966

President Lyndon Johnson signs a truth-in-packaging law that requires manufacturers of prepared foods to identify ingredients on the label. *Nutrition Action*, a monthly health newsletter published by the Center for Science in the Public Interest, contains useful food label information as well as food and fitness tips. Their Web site is *www.cspinet.org*.

Investigate

Compare the ingredients of several foods and discuss their nutritional values.

NOVEMBER 4

1849

Along with six other families, Catherine Haun and her husband leave Clinton, Iowa, to look for gold in California. They reach Sacramento six months and ten days later.

Investigate

Find Clinton, Iowa, on the map and trace a route to Sacramento. About how many miles is it? How many miles a day, on average, does the Haun family travel?

1880

James and John Ritty, of Dayton, Ohio, patent the cash register.

Investigate

Suppose a cash register drawer contains five twenty-dollar bills, twice as many tens as twenties, three times as many fives as tens, and five times as many ones as fives. How much money is in the cash register?

Make up a problem like this for others to solve.

Make up problems like this that all produce the answer of $500.00.

NOVEMBER 5

1895

A patent is issued to George Selden for the gasoline-driven automobile.

Investigate
Check the odometer of your family car(s) one morning and write the figure(s) down. At the same time a week later, check the odometer(s) again, writing down the new figure(s). Combine the number of miles driven with those driven by your classmates' families and project a probable total for the year.

1963

John and Frank Craighead track a bear into hibernation. They name her Marian, weigh her (she weighs 125 pounds), and put a collar on her that transmits a radio signal (so they are able to track her). A year later Marian has gained 175 pounds.

Investigate
Mental Math: What did Marian weigh a year later?

NOVEMBER 6

1854

John Philip Sousa, future composer, band conductor, and inventor of the sousaphone, is born.

Investigate
Marches are written in 4/4 time. Waltzes are written in 3/4 time. Find out about these and other time signatures.

John Philip Sousa is born on November 6, 1854

Count an octave on a piano. Count the number of black keys and white keys. What is the total number of keys? They are all Fibonacci numbers.

1986

Cecilia Rubio wins the American Pie Contest, in Nashville, Tennessee. Her entry is a lemon meringue pie.

Investigate
Bring a pie recipe to class. Rewrite the ingredients to make a pie that will serve the entire class; the whole school.

How many pieces are created by two straight cuts across a pie? How about by four cuts? seven? Is there a pattern?

NOVEMBER 7

1504

Christopher Columbus, age 53, returns home after his fourth and most difficult voyage. His 13-year-old son, Ferdinand, sailed with him. (Ferdinand had plenty of company his own age. A third of the crew were between 12 and 18.) Upon his return, Columbus writes a letter of complaint to King Ferdinand and Queen Isabella of Spain, pointing out that he has served them since he was 28 and he feels he should be better treated.

Investigate
Mental Math: What year did Columbus begin serving the king and queen of Spain?

1986

An eight-foot-tall fiberglass statue of Superman is dedicated in Metropolis, Illinois.

Investigate
Along with your classmates, draw an eight-foot-tall figure on butcher paper. (Choose a superhero, a real hero, a favorite character from a book, whomever you like.) Predict where the top of your head will come on this eight-foot-tall figure. Then hang the figure in an accessible place, and have every student in the class mark his or her height on the figure with a self-adhesive tab bearing the student's name. What do you notice? Where are most of the labels clustered?

NOVEMBER 8

1656

English astronomer and mathematician Edmond Halley is born in London, England. Halley observed the great comet of 1682 and calculated the regular periods of its orbit, figuring out that the comets observed in 1531 and 1607 were this same comet. He correctly predicted it would be seen again around 1758. The Halley comet was most recently visible in 1986, when it again reached the spot in its seventy-six-year elliptical orbit where it is closest to the Sun.

Investigate
When will the Halley comet again be visible?

1731

In Philadelphia, Benjamin Franklin opens the first subscription library in the United States. Members donate money to buy books and then use the books free of charge. According to research at Indiana University, the average woman reads 164 minutes a day, the average man 150 minutes. Research at MIT indicates the average American reads 8,500 words a day.

Investigate
Come up with your own reading statistics: How many pages do you and your classmates read a day? How much time do you spend reading? Graph the results.

Have a friend time you reading aloud a page from a book and then reading it to yourself. Compare the two times.

NOVEMBER 9

1936

The giant panda is discovered, in China. The giant panda is a cross between a bear and a raccoon and its habitat is the bamboo jungles on mountainous land between China and Tibet. In three days a giant panda eats 240 pounds of bamboo.

Investigate
Estimate how many pounds of food a dog eats in three days. How does this compare with the giant panda's 240 pounds?

1965

The biggest power failure ever strikes seven northeastern states and Ontario, Canada. About 30 million people in an area covering 80,000 square miles are without electrical power for $13\frac{1}{2}$ hours.

Investigate
As a class, make a list of all the things you do at home that require electricity. Then

divide the things on your list into essential and nonessential categories.

Keep an hourly electricity chart at home that notes where electricity is being used.

NOVEMBER 10
1896

Ernst Paul Heinz Prüfer is born in Germany. A mathematician, he works on knot theory, which is a branch of topology. Scientists use the mathematics of knots to understand the links of DNA, the molecules that determine the genetic code of every living thing. Mathematicians try to distinguish between true knots and tangles that come apart (and are called *unknots*). They put knots into groups of how many times a string crosses itself.

Investigate
Experiment with different types of knots and unknots. How can you tell which is which? Count the number of times string crosses itself in the knots you find.

1967

The Census Bureau issues a statement that the population of the United States is now 200 million people. It has doubled in fifty years. You can check out the Census Bureau online at *http://www.census.gov.*

Investigate
What is the U.S. population today? How much has it grown in thirty years?

NOVEMBER 11
1949

A rare plankton-feeding whale shark is captured off the Baba Island near Karachi, Pakistan. The shark measures $41\frac{1}{2}$ feet long and 23 feet around the thickest part of the body. It weighs an estimated 18 tons. We are more familiar with the great white shark, the largest predatory fish, averaging between 14 and 15 feet long and weighing between 1,150 and 1,700 pounds.

Investigate
What fraction of this whale shark's size is the great white shark?

1997

The *Rotterdam* VI, a Holland America long-haul liner, sets out from Fort Lauderdale, Florida, on its maiden voyage. The liner, which can cruise at 25 knots, is 780 feet long and weighs 62,000 gross tons. It can accommodate 1,316 passengers on its ten decks. The price per day for a 70-day around-the-world cruise on this ship ranges from $240 to $490.

Investigate
Mental Math: What's the most and least it could cost for the 70-day cruise?

NOVEMBER 12
1956

The U.S.S. *Glacier* sights a tabular (flat-surfaced) iceberg 208 miles long and 60 miles wide 150 miles west of Scott Island, in the South Pacific.

Investigate
How does the area of the iceberg compare with the area of your state? Of the United States?

1997

The annual Christmas tree arrives at New York City's Rockefeller Center. It is 74 feet tall and weighs 7 tons. The 74-foot Norway Spruce, which was planted in Richfield, Ohio, in 1938, arrives at Kennedy Airport. This is the first Rockefeller Center Christmas tree flown to

November 1997 — Rockefeller Center in New York City

New York (it would have been a logistical nightmare to drive a 20-foot-wide tree on interstate highways at 25 miles per hour).

Investigate
Mental Math: How old was the Ohio tree when it was cut down?

NOVEMBER 13

1946

Vincent Joseph Schaefer, an employee of the General Electric Company, flies over Mt. Greylock, Massachusetts, dispenses small dry-ice pellets into a cloud at a height of 14,000 feet, and produces artificial snow. The snow falls for about 3,000 feet, but

because of the dry atmosphere below the cloud, the snow evaporates before reaching the ground.

For a biography of the snowflake photographer who inspired the 1999 Caldecott book *Snowflake Bentley* and spectacular photos of snowflakes, go to *http://www .snowflakebentley.com*.

Investigate
Research snowflakes and then cut out symmetric paper snowflakes. How many lines of symmetry are there in a snowflake?

1980

Voyager 1 approaches Saturn. The distance the space ship has traveled is mind-boggling. Jupiter is 3,000 times farther away from Earth than the moon is, and Saturn is 6,000 times farther away than Jupiter. You can make this trip online at *http://pds.jpl.nasa.gov/planets* and *http://seds.lpl.arizona.edu/nineplanets /nineplanets/nineplanets.html*.

Investigate

How far did *Voyager* travel to reach Saturn?

NOVEMBER 14

1941

Author Daniel Pinkwater is born. In Pinkwater's story *The Hoboken Chicken Emergency*, Arthur's mother sends him to the store for a chicken. He gets the best poultry bargain ever—a 266-pound super chicken, for six cents a pound. The seller lends Arthur a collar and leash so he can get the chicken home.

Investigate

How much did Arthur pay for this super chicken?

1972

For the first time in its 76-year history, the Dow Jones industrial average closes above the 1,000 mark: 1003.16. For information about Dow Jones averages, check *www.cftech .com/BrainBank/FINANCE/DowJonesAvgsHist .html* or *www.e-analytics.com/f13.htm*.

Investigate

When did the Dow Jones industrial average begin reporting?

Check the Dow Jones industrial average today. How many times has it grown?

NOVEMBER 15

1869

Free delivery of the mail begins in San Francisco. The city's inhabitants had previously been charged three or four dollars for each piece of mail they received.

Investigate

Count the pieces of mail delivered to your house in one week. If you had to pay $3.50 for each piece, how much would you owe?

**The Hoboken Chicken Emergency
November, 1941**

1926

Jennie and Jack, a giraffe couple living in New York's Bronx Zoo, become the proud parents of a son. "Shorty" measures 5 feet, 9 inches at birth. Infant giraffes fall about five feet to the ground when they are born. This fall starts them breathing. The giraffe is the world's tallest animal. An adult male may grow as tall as 18 feet (5.5 meters).

Investigate

Find out your own length at birth and compare it with your height today.

Compare a human being's rate of growth from birth to adulthood with a giraffe's.

NOVEMBER 16

1907

Oklahoma becomes the 46th state.

Investigate

Mental Math: How long ago did Oklahoma become a state?

1958

Six inches of snow fall on Tucson, Arizona, catching autumn golfers by surprise.

Investigate

Mental Math: How long ago did this occur?

Investigate snowfall records for your area. Display the results in a graph.

NOVEMBER 17

1869

The Suez Canal formally opens on this day. The 101-mile (163 kilometers) canal connects the Mediterranean and Red Seas, eliminating a trip around Africa of about 4000 miles.

Investigate

Mental Math: How many years ago did the Suez Canal open?

About how many times longer is the trip around Africa than the trip through the canal?

1889

Through railroad service begins between Chicago and Portland, Oregon, and between Chicago and San Francisco. Passengers no longer have to change trains in Omaha.

Investigate

Which of the two trips was longer? By how much?

NOVEMBER 18

1805

A California condor is killed on the Lewis and Clark expedition. The condor is the largest extant bird—50 inches long with a wingspan of up to ten feet. Once on the verge of extinction, the condor, with the help of conservationists, began to make a comeback in the Grand Canyon in the late 1990s.

Investigate

Compare the condor's wingspan-to-length ratio with that of several styles of airplanes.

1820

Captain Nathaniel Brown Palmer, sailing in the *Hero*, a 44-ton sloop with a crew of six, discovers Antarctica, at a point near latitude 64 degrees south and longitude 60 degrees west. The ship sailed from Stonington, Connecticut, on July 25, 1820, and returned May 8, 1821.

Investigate

How long was the crew at sea?

Chart a probable route from Connecticut to Antarctica.

NOVEMBER 19

1916

At 7:20 A.M., Ruth Low begins her attempt to fly from Grant Park, on the Lake Michigan shore in Chicago, to New York City in one day, a feat that has never been done. She flies 590 miles nonstop, then runs out of gas and lands, at 2 P.M. She refuels and takes off again at 3:24 P.M. She then runs into difficulty and doesn't reach New York City until the next day. However, her 590-mile nonstop flight still set a record.

Investigate
Look at a map and figure out where Low might have made her 2 P.M. landing.

1997

Septuplets are born in Des Moines, Iowa. Proctor and Gamble says their offer of a lifetime supply of Pampers will amount to roughly 31,500 disposable diapers.

Investigate
Assuming a baby wears diapers for two years, how many diapers did Proctor and Gamble figure a baby wears each day?

NOVEMBER 20

1819

The three-masted whaling ship Essex is rammed head on by a huge sperm whale. The whale goes under the ship, turns, and rams it again, sinking it. By the time the crew members were rescued 83 days later, only eight were still alive. Some years later, Herman Melville heard this "wondrous story"; his epic novel Moby-Dick was published in 1851.

Investigate
What day were the eight crew members rescued?

1866

The rotary-crank bicycle, know as the bone shaker, is patented by Pierre Lallemont in Paris, France.

Investigate
Mental Math: How old is the invention of the bicycle?

Poll your classmates about their bicycles. Choose one aspect to explore—manufacturer, color, diameter of wheels, height of handlebars, etc.—and graph the data you collect.

NOVEMBER 21

1787

Eight-year-old Peter Mark Roget makes his first entry in his notebook. He goes on to create *Roget's Thesaurus*. Roget's lifelong passion for collecting and categorizing words was passed on to his son and grandson, who continued to update his famous work. You can visit a thesaurus online at *http ://humanities.uchicago.edu/forms_unrest/ROGET .html* and *http//www.thesaurus.com*.

Investigate
For one week, keep a vocabulary journal of words you encounter that are new to you. Compile the data from your class into a graph.

1789

North Carolina becomes the 12th of the 13 original colonies to join the United States of America.

Investigate
Mental Math: How long ago did North Carolina become a state?

NOVEMBER 22

1682

Edmond Halley sees the comet that later bears his name. Halley figured out that the comets observed earlier in 1531 and 1607 were actually this same comet. He predicted it would be seen again around 1758. When it appeared on schedule, the comet was named in his honor.

Investigate

How many times has the Halley comet traveled around the Sun since 240 B.C.?

1990

Led by Yevgeniu Lepechov, a team of eleven people in Chernigov, Kiev, Ukraine,

finish building a pyramid containing 362,194 bottle caps. Ron Werner, of Bothell, Washington, has a collection of 6,352 different bottles from 71 countries, of which 3,235 are full. On February 14, 1995, ten science students of University College, in Dublin, Belfield, Ireland, build a pyramid of 5,525 empty cans in 30 minutes. On August 16, 1995, ten students from Nakamura Elementary School, in Yokohama, Japan, tie the record.

Investigate

Mental Math: Are more or less than half of the bottles in Ron Werner's collection full?

How long would it take your class to collect 362,194 bottle caps or 5,525 cans?

1531
1607
1682
1758

Edmond Halley sees a comet.
November 1682

NOVEMBER 23

1835

Henry Burden, of Troy, New York, patents a machine that can produce 60 horseshoes a minute. Most of the horseshoes for the Union cavalry during the Civil War were made in Troy.

Investigate
How many horses can this machine make shoes for in one hour?

1899

The jukebox, invented by Louis Glass, debuts in San Francisco, California.

Investigate
Assume you want to play three songs on a jukebox. In what order could you listen to them? How do you know you've found all the possible sequences? What happens when you add a fourth song?

NOVEMBER 24

1847

When she is not allowed to take an anatomy class, medical student Elizabeth Blackwell writes a note to the professor stating her serious purpose as a medical student and her need to study anatomy. The professor reads her note to the all-male class, and they vote to let her attend. Blackwell graduates two years later and becomes the first woman doctor in the United States. But her troubles aren't over: landlords won't rent her office space, and other doctors shun her.

Investigate
Research the percentage of medical students today who are women.

1930

Ruth Nichols takes off from Mineola, Long Island, New York, in a Lockheed-Vega air-

plane. She arrives at Burbank, California, on December 1, completing the first transcontinental airplane flight by a woman. Her total flying time is 16 hours, 59 minutes, 30 seconds.

Investigate
What was Nichols's approximate speed per hour?

NOVEMBER 25

1919

Charles Stillwell dies. In 1883 he invented a machine to produce brown paper grocery bags. These days, Americans use 40 billion paper grocery bags a year.

Investigate
Keep track of the number of grocery bags your family brings home in a week. Bring the information to class and organize a class graph.

1984

The "first lady" of space dies. On May 29, 1959, Miss Baker, an eleven-ounce, two-year-old squirrel monkey, a native of Iquitos, Peru, blasted off from Cape Canaveral in the nose cone of a *Jupiter* rocket. Her companion was a seven-pound rhesus monkey named Able. Scientists wanted to study the effects of space travel on this pair. They traveled 1700 miles, achieved an altitude of 350 miles, and a speed of over 10,000 miles per hour. They withstood forces 38 times the pull of gravity. Splashdown occurred 90 minutes after liftoff. After her flight Miss Baker lived at the School of Aviation Medicine, in Pensacola, Florida, for nineteen years and then moved to the Alabama Space and Rocket Center, in Huntsville. She received fan mail from children from all over the country.

Investigate
Mental Math: How old was Miss Baker when she died?

NOVEMBER 26

1620

Miles Standish and William Bradford find corn growing near what is now Provincetown, Massachusetts. This corn probably means the difference between the colonists' starving and surviving. These days, we tend to think of corn as a snack food, not as a necessity of life. Students at the Beauclerc Elementary School, in Jacksonville, Florida, thought about nothing but popcorn for five days, and had loads of fun doing it. They made the world's largest box of popcorn. The container was 39 feet, $11\frac{1}{2}$ inches long; 20 feet, $8\frac{1}{2}$ inches wide; and 8 feet high. Every classroom in the school had a hot-air popper going all the time.

Investigate
How many cubic feet of popcorn did it take to fill this box?

Pop a batch of popcorn. How many batches the same size will it take to fill one cubic foot?

1997

Charles Schulz, cartoonist of Snoopy fame, celebrates his 75th birthday by taking a five-week holiday from cartooning chores. The *Peanuts* comic strip premiered on October 2, 1950. Syndicated by United Feature Syndicate, it appears in 2,400 newspapers and is translated into 26 languages.

As a young boy sitting in his father's barbershop, Charles read an article about Frank King, who drew the comic strip *Gasoline Alley*. It said that King made 1,000 dollars a week. Charles told his father, "That's what I'm going to do. I'm going to draw a comic strip and I'm going to earn 1,000 dollars a week." Schulz died in February 2000.

Investigate
Mental Math: How old was Schulz when Snoopy first appeared?

Popping corn in Jacksonville, Florida

NOVEMBER 27

1702

Anders Celsius, future astronomer who will invent the centigrade (or Celsius) scale, is born. Years ago Congress legislated that the United States would use the metric standard, including Celsius temperature designations, but it has never been put into practice. The United States is one of the very few countries in the world that does not use the metric system.

Investigate
One way to become familiar with a new measuring system is to use it. Keep track of the temperature in Celsius notation for one month. What's the average temperature for the month?

1976

Popular author-illustrator Steven Kellogg acquires Pinkerton, the huge dog that becomes the model for his books of the same name.

Investigate
Read a number of these books and figure out how big Pinkerton is.

NOVEMBER 28

1895

The first automobile race in America is held with six cars traveling from Jackson Park in Chicago to Waukegan, Illinois. J. Frank Dureyea wins, traveling at $7\frac{1}{2}$ miles per hour! It took him 7 hours, 53 minutes to make the trek (bathroom stops not included). He won $2,000 for the effort.

Investigate
How far was the race?

How long would it take today to drive that distance at thirty miles per hour? forty miles per hour? fifty miles per hour?

1984

McDonald's sells its 50-billionth hamburger. The company's restaurants around the world sell about 140 hamburgers every second. According to environmentalists, it takes 45,000 liters of water to produce one pound of hamburger. Most of that water is used for growing the feed for the cows.

Investigate
How many McDonald's hamburgers are sold in a day? in a month?

NOVEMBER 29

1959

The Grammy Awards are shown on network television for the first time. (It is actually the second year of the Grammy Awards.)

Investigate
Mental Math: How many years have Grammy Awards been given?

1973

A Ruppell's vulture collides with a commercial airplane over Bidjan, Ivory Coast, damaging one of the plane's engines, but the plane is able to land safely. Experts at the Museum of Natural History in Washington, D.C., are able to identify the bird from feather remains on the plane. The plane was at an altitude of 37,000 feet, thus documenting that vultures can fly this high.

Investigate
How many miles high was this vulture flying?

1986

By the end of the 24-hour BirdWatch Kenya event, Terry Stevenson, John Fanshawe, and Andy Roberts have spotted 342 species of birds, the greatest number of species spotted in a 24-hour period. In the thirty years she has been watching birds, Phoebe Snetsinger, of Webster Groves, Missouri, has seen 8,040 of the 9,700 known species.

Investigate

How many different bird sightings does Phoebe Snetsinger average a year?

1991

A statue of Ramses II, who died in 1225 B.C., is found by Egyptian construction workers 300 miles south of Cairo, Egypt.

Investigate

How old is this statue today, assuming it was sculpted the year Ramses II died?

DECEMBER

DECEMBER 1

1913

The world's first drive-in gas station opens for business, in Pittsburgh. On opening day it sells 30 gallons of gas. Today, one 747-400 airplane has a fuel capacity of 57,285 gallons.

Investigate

How many 20-gallon car fill-ups does it take to equal one 747-400 fill-up?

What is the effect of a five-cent-per-gallon price increase on fuel on a car fill-up? On the 747-400?

1987

Work begins on the English Channel Tunnel. Fifteen thousand workers remove more than 9.1 million cubic yards of soil. The Channel Tunnel is 31 miles (50 kilometers) long and links the railroads of France and England. Special electric trains have been running through the tunnel since 1994. Three tunnels lie 150 feet (45 meters) below the seabed. Trains run in opposite directions in the two large tunnels. A third, smaller tunnel is for safety access. *Le Shuttle* makes 20 trips a day. It can carry 120 cars, 12 buses, and 1,000 passengers.

Investigate

Looking at all these statistics, write a paragraph about the one you find most remarkable. Explain why.

DECEMBER 2

1816

The Philadelphia Saving Fund Society becomes the first bank to receive money on deposit when it opens for business on this day.

Investigate

How much money will a depositor earn in one year on a $100 deposit earning 5 percent?

1992

At Beale Air Force base in California, Lou Scripa, Jr., completes his 70,715th sit-up, 24 hours after he does the first one.

Investigate

How many sit-ups did Lou Scripa do per minute on average?

DECEMBER 3

1621

Galileo invents the telescope. You can view the wonders of the solar system online at http://www.nasa.gov.

Investigate

Mental Math: How long ago was the telescope invented?

1984

A white rhinoceros named Zimba is born at the London Zoo, a thirty-six-acre conservation center in Regent's Park. A rhino's life span is, on average, 25 years. An adult rhino can grow to be up to 14 feet (4.3 meters) long.

In the 1980s, fewer than twenty white rhinos survive; in 1994, they were second in the World Wildlife Federation's "Top Ten

Most Endangered Species" list. In 2000, the conservation of black and white rhinos is still a top priority. For more information see http://www.worldwildlife.org.

Investigate

Research rhino facts and create a birth announcement.

Mental Math: What year is Zimba likely to die?

Identify three things that are about 14 feet long.

DECEMBER 4

1766

At Fort Ticonderoga, New York, leaders of the revolutionary forces tell the Continental Congress that there are only 900 pairs of shoes for more than 12,000 soldiers.

Investigate

Mental Math: About how many of these soldiers will be without shoes?

1983

A new Jewish Theological Seminary library is dedicated, in New York City. On April 18, 1966, 85,000 of the library's 250,000 books, many of them ancient and irreplaceable, were lost in a fire. The rest of the books were saved by people in the neighborhood. Hundreds of volunteers, from kindergarten children to corporate CEOs, formed a chain and passed the books out of the building into the hands of people who knew how to dry water-soaked pages.

Investigate

Mental Math: How many books were saved from the fire?

New York City

DECEMBER 5

1880

Levi Strauss invents blue jeans.

Investigate
Good ideas catch on. Check how many brands of jeans the kids in your classroom are wearing and graph the results.

1955

In Montgomery, Alabama, following Rosa Park's arrest for refusing to give up her seat on the bus, a then-unknown Baptist minister, Martin Luther King, Jr., organizes a bus boycott. The boycott lasts 382 days. There are numerous children's books about Rosa Parks's brave deed, including *Rosa Parks: My Story.*

Investigate
What day did the boycott end? Discuss your methods for figuring this out.

DECEMBER 6

1884

The capstone, with its aluminum tip, is set on the Washington Monument in Washington D.C. The monument is a white marble obelisk 555 feet tall and 55 feet square at the base. The cornerstone was laid July 4, 1848, and the monument was dedicated February 21, 1885. Information about the monument is online at *http://www .nps.gov/wamo.*

Investigate
Mental Math: How many years elapsed between laying the cornerstone and setting the capstone?

Compare this monument's height with that of the Great Pyramid at Giza, which is 481 feet (147 meters) high, and the Eiffel Tower, in Paris, which is 1,052 feet (321 meters) tall.

How high is your classroom ceiling? If your school height was equal to the height of the

Washington Monument, how many floors would it have?

1902

An eight-cent stamp honoring Martha Washington is issued, making her the first American woman to appear on a U.S. stamp.

Investigate
Mental Math: How many eight-cent stamps will it take to mail a first-class letter today? How many calories would you expend licking those stamps? (The average stamp lick consumes 5.9 calories.)

DECEMBER 7

1941

The first television newscast, broadcast by CBS, is a report of the Japanese raid on Pearl Harbor.

Investigate
Analyze a day of television programming. What fraction or percent consists of news? Sitcoms? Movies? Other categories of programs?

1968

Richard Dodd returns a book on febrile diseases checked out by his great grandfather from the University of Cincinnati Medical Library in 1823. The fine, $2,254, is waived.

Investigate
Mental Math: How many years has this book been overdue? What fine was charged for each overdue day?

DECEMBER 8

1765

Eli Whitney, future inventor and manufacturer, is born in Westboro, Massachusetts. While visiting a friend in Georgia, Whitney became interested in the way cotton was picked and processed. He noticed that it took a whole day to clean the sticky seeds from the fibers of just one pound of cotton. Whitney invented a machine to clean the cotton mechanically. He got a patent for the "cotton gin" in 1794.

Investigate
Mental Math: How many years have passed since Eli Whitney's birth?

1831

James Hoban, Irish-born architect of the White House, dies. Blueprints are available (free to teachers) from the White House Liaison, National Park Service, 1100 Ohio Drive, SW, Washington, DC 20242. You can visit the White House online at *http://www.whitehouse.gov/WH/kids/html/home.html.*

Investigate
What are the dimensions of some of the rooms in the White House? Which room is closest in size to your classroom?

DECEMBER 9

1901

A paired six-day bicycle race begins at New York's Madison Square Garden. (Paired races started when a law was passed earlier that year forbidding one rider to be on the track for more than twelve hours a day.) The winners of this race pedal 2,555 miles and win $1,500.

Investigate
Mental Math: If they share this prize, how much does each rider receive?

How many miles did these bikers average a day?

1994

The asteroid 1994XM, 33 feet in diameter, is discovered, by James Scotti of the United States, 14 hours before it passes within 62,000 miles of Earth.

Investigate
On the playground or in the gym, draw a circle of 33 feet in diameter.

What is an asteroid? Would you know an asteroid if you saw one?

DECEMBER 10

1830

Emily Dickinson, who grew up to become a reclusive poet, is born in Amherst, Massachusetts. At school Emily was known for her sense of fun and for her wit, but after leaving South Hadley Female Seminary, now Mount Holyoke, she almost never left home. She lived a quiet life and wrote 1,500 poems. She died in 1886.

To learn more about Dickinson, visit the Emily Dickinson International Society site: *www.cwru.edu/affil/edis/edisindex.html*.

Investigate
How many poems, on average, did Emily write a year if she started writing them at age 20?

1851

Melvil Dewey, future American librarian and inventor of the Dewey decimal book classification system, is born at Adams Center, New York. Dewey bases his system on numbers from 000 to 999—with decimals in between. Dewey is also credited with inventing the vertical office file.

Sixth graders have created an informative Dewey decimal site at *http://tqjunior .thinkquest.org/5002*.

Investigate
Which category do you think has the most books: the one that starts with zero? The 100s? 200s? First find out what books are in each category, then guess, then go to your school library to check.

DECEMBER 11

1928

Inventor Lewis Latimer dies. As a young man, Latimer, who was black, was a top draftsman for a group of patent lawyers. When Alexander Graham Bell, inventor of the telephone, needed drawings for his patent application, Latimer prepared them. Latimer was very interested in Edison's lightbulb. He invented ways to improve Edison's lamp and joined Edison's company, serving as Edison's chief draftsman.

Investigate
Invite a draftsman to speak to your class about the requirements of drafting.

1946

The United Nations International Children's Emergency Fund (UNICEF) is created by the United Nations General Assembly.

For information about their current work, see *http://www.unicefusa.org*.

Investigate
Mental Math: How old is UNICEF?

DECEMBER 12
1866

George Parker, future game manufacturer, is born. In 1990, the top children's games are Uno, Monopoly, Bicycle Playing Cards, Yahtzee, and Candy Land.

Investigate
Categorize board games you have played into three lists: games of chance, games of skill, and games that involve both chance and skill.

1925

The first motel in the United States opens, in San Luis Obispo, California.

Investigate
Mental Math: How many years ago did the first motel open?

George Parker is born on December 12, 1866.

DECEMBER 13
1577

British explorer Sir Francis Drake sets out on a voyage to the Pacific Ocean. He reaches it September 6, 1578.

Investigate
How many days did it take Drake to reach the Pacific?

1904

Italo Marchiony, an Italian immigrant, receives a patent on his ice cream cone mold. According to the Human Nutrition Information Service, nearly 25 percent of all Americans have eaten ice cream at least once in the last three days. According to the International Association of Ice Cream Manufacturers, 84 percent of American households eat ice cream at least once a month. The four most popular flavors, in descending order, are (1) vanilla, (2) chocolate, (3) neapoliltan, and (4) strawberry.

Investigate
Verify the above figures by taking your own poll of how often people eat ice cream and what their favorite flavors are. Display the information you gather in a graph.

DECEMBER 14
1962

When Leonardo da Vinci's *La Gioconda* (the Mona Lisa) is lent by the Louvre in Paris for display first in Washington, D.C., and then in New York City, the painting is valued at $100 million. You can visit the painting online at the Louvre at *http://sunsite.unc.edu/louvre*.

Investigate
Write the number 100 million in scientific notation (for example, 6,000 is 6×10^3).

1985

A real gingerbread house is built at New York's Rockefeller Center. This house is big enough for people to walk through.

Investigate
Assume the floor of this house was half the size of your classroom floor. How many $8\frac{1}{2}$-inch-by-11-inch pieces of gingerbread did it take to construct the walls and roof?

DECEMBER 15

1887

Inventor Andrew Jackson Beard sells his patent on a plow he invented for $5,200. Ten years later, he figured out a way to couple railroad cars automatically. Before this, men had to run along the top of a freight train, climb down between the two cars, and insert a pin as the cars come together. It was very dangerous work.

Investigate
The first transcontinental railroad is finished in 1869. How many years did men have to couple the cars by hand?

1981

American households receive an average of 59 mail-order catalogs. Ten years later, in 1991, they are receiving 142 catalogs per household.

Investigate
Keep a record of catalogs that arrive at your house each day for a week. Bring your total to class to compare with your classmates. Based on the data you collect, make an estimate of how many catalogs a household today receives in a year.

DECEMBER 16

1773

To protest British taxes on tea, patriots disguised as Mohawk Indians board three British ships in Boston Harbor and dump 350 chests of tea overboard. Patriots say they don't want to pay taxes when they have no vote. This has since become a celebrated event, but colonial leaders such as John Adams and George Washington denounced this destruction of private property as mob violence. Samuel Adams, John's cousin, was much more of a firebrand.

Investigate
Keep a chart of the items your family buys in a week that are and are not taxed. What percentage are taxed? Not taxed? Bring your data to class and compare with your classmates.

Why do you think that some items, such as gasoline, have higher taxes than other items?

1902

The National Biscuit Company introduces Barnum's Animal Crackers. The box has a white string so it can be hung on a Christmas tree. A box of 20 crackers contains a mixture of lions, buffaloes, polar bears, camels, hippos, rhinos, gorillas, panthers, zebras, elephants, tigers, and giraffes.

In 1993, people in the United States eat 12.29 pounds of cookies and crackers per capita. People in the Netherlands eat 58.28 pounds per capita.

Investigate
What mixtures of animals are possible in a box of 20 animal crackers? How many different assortments can you find so each box has at least one of each animal?

If you had 12 pounds of your favorite cookies, about how many individual cookies would there be?

DECEMBER 17
1790

A 25-ton stone Aztec calendar, carved in the 15th century, is found buried in Mexico City. The Aztec calendar uses a 260-day year. The Mayan calendar is similar: although it uses a year of 365 days, the days are divided into eighteen 20-day periods, with a 5-day period at the end. The French Revolutionary calendar, instituted in 1793, is divided into 12 months of 30 days. It has no weeks but divides each month into three 10-day periods. The months' names are descriptive: fog month, sleet month, and so on through snow, rain, wind, seed, blossom, pasture, harvest, heat, fruit, and vintage.

Investigate
How old would you be if you had been born in a society that uses a 260-day year?

1947

The first episode of *Howdy Doody* is telecast, on NBC. The show airs five times a week. There were a total of 2,743 episodes.

Investigate
If there were 12 weeks of reruns each year, what year did *Howdy Doody* go off the air?

DECEMBER 18
1965

Gemini 7 touches down in the Atlantic Ocean after circling Earth 206 times. Astronauts Frank Borman and James Lovell have been in flight for 330 hours, 35 minutes. *Gemini* 6 has been orbiting Earth at the same time. At one point, 185 miles (298 kilometers) above Earth, *Gemini* 7 and *Gemini* 6 rendezvous

within one foot (30 centimeters) of each other and fly in formation for 20 hours.

Investigate
What day was *Gemini* 7 launched?

1987

Kids' favorite games are reported to be *Pictionary*, *Nintendo*, and the *Real Ghostbusters*.

Investigate
What are this year's three favorites among your classmates? Take a poll, graph the results, and report your conclusions.

DECEMBER 19
1732

Benjamin Franklin publishes *Poor Richard's Almanac*. It contains famous aphorisms, such as "Early to bed and early to rise makes a man healthy, wealthy, and wise," that are still quoted today.

A site with lots of information about this talented man is *http://sln.fi.edu/franklin /rotten.html*.

Investigate
Mental Math: How old is *Poor Richard's Almanac*?

1958

The U.S. Earth satellite *Atlas* transmits the first radio voice broadcast from space, a 58-word greeting from President Dwight Eisenhower.

Investigate
About how many letters would there be in a 58-word message?

Create a 58-word message to send to outer space. (What words would you want to be the first to reach a civilization other than Earth?) Then count the letters. Compare messages and the number of letters with your classmates. What does this exploration tell you about the lengths of words?

DECEMBER 20

1790

Samuel Slater, of Pawtucket, Rhode Island, operates the first cotton mill able to spin cotton yarn successfully. The mill is 40 feet long, 26 feet wide, and two stories high.

Investigate
Estimate a distance of 40 feet, and then measure to find out how accurate you were.

1843

Charles Dickens's *Christmas Carol*, published yesterday, has already sold 6,000 copies. When Dickens later visited the United States, people in New York City lined up for a mile to get an autographed copy of one of his books.

Investigate
Come up with a way to determine how many people are in a mile-long line.

DECEMBER 21

1620

Dr. Samuel Fuller, one of the signers of the compact drawn up on board the *Mayflower*, arrives at Plymouth, Massachusetts, along with 102 other Pilgrims. He is the only physician in the colony. You can visit the Mayflower online at *http://members.aol.com /calebj/mayflower.html*.

Investigate
Count the number of physicians listed in the yellow pages of your local telephone book and then figure out the people-to-doctor ratio for your area.

1872

Phileas Fogg completes his (fictitious) around-the-world trip in Jules Verne's most successful novel, *Around the World in 80 Days*.

Investigate
What day did Phileas Fogg set off on his trip?

DECEMBER 22

1943

Three-year-old Jennifer Land asks, "Why can't I see them now?" after her father, Edwin Land, has taken a number of photographs. Her question sets him thinking about instant photographs, and the idea for the camera, the film, and the physical chemistry for processing the film became clear to him within an hour. The result was the Polaroid Land Camera, christened Model 95 because it sold for 95 dollars. Although a Kodak Baby Brownie sold for $2.75 in 1949, when the Model 95 went on sale in 1943, people bought it as fast as it could be produced.

Investigate
How many Baby Brownies could you have bought for the money needed to buy one Polaroid Land Camera?

1943

What do Polaroid cameras cost today? How do today's prices compare with the 1943 price of Model 95?

1956

At the Columbus Zoo, in Ohio, Christina produces 3.25-pound Colo; Christina is the world's first captive gorilla to give birth. When Christina seems confused by the strange arrival, Colo is hand-reared by humans. A second captive gorilla birth occurs at the Basel Zoo, in Switzerland, on September 22, 1959. This gorilla is also hand-reared. The Lincoln Park Zoo, in Chicago, has the most successful gorilla breeding program in the world. Since 1970, 38 gorillas have been born at Lincoln Park, 15 percent of captive gorilla births in North America. In 1976, the zoo built the Lester E. Fisher Great Ape House so that the gorillas could live in troops as they would in the wild.

In 1984 the American Association of Zoos began a Species Survival Plan for the western lowland gorilla. Forty-seven zoos housing over 200 gorillas agreed to participate.

Investigate

If 47 zoos house 200 gorillas, how many gorillas, on average, are in each zoo?

Compare your own birth weight with Colo's, and compare the probable weight of her mother with that of human women.

DECEMBER 23

1975

Congress passes the Metric Conversion Act, declaring that the metric system will be the nation's system of measurement.

Investigate

"Go metric" in your classroom: measure the length of at least ten things using centime-ters. For each, make an estimate first, then measure.

Write to your representatives in Congress and ask them what happened to the Metric Conversion Act.

1987

Dick Rutan and Jeana Yeager set a new world record of 216 hours of continuous flight around the world without refueling. They cover 24,986 miles at an official speed of 115 miles an hour.

Investigate

What day did Rutan and Yeager start this trip?

Why do you think they kept to this relatively low speed?

DECEMBER 24

1895

George Vanderbilt travels to his new home in Biltmore, North Carolina. He doesn't want any close neighbors, so he has purchased 146,000 acres (22 square miles). His 250-room mansion measures 780 feet across the front. The largest room in the house is the banquet hall, which measures 12 feet by 42 feet and has a 70-foot ceiling.

Investigate

How many rooms are in your school? How does this compare with the mansion's rooms?

DECEMBER 25

1492

Just after midnight, the *Santa Maria*, one of the three ships on Columbus's voyage, hits a coral reef off Haiti. It is a calm night and so Columbus has gone to sleep. The sailor steering the ship also decided to take a snooze, leaving the steering to a boy. The *Santa Maria* was beyond saving, and the crew built a fort from beams of the wrecked ship. This became the first Christian settlement on these shores; Columbus calls it La Navidad.

Investigate
Mental Math: How many years ago was this early settlement built?

DECEMBER 26
1833

Seth Fuller, of Boston, Massachusetts, receives a patent for the annunciator, installed at Tremont House, Boston, Massachusetts. Known as "the hanging bells," it consists of 140 bells that occupy a space 57 feet long, 6 feet high, and 1 foot deep.

Investigate
Put differing amounts of water in a number of water glasses and then use a metal object to clink the side of each glass. Develop a theory about the relationship of the amount of water to the tone produced.

1966

Kwanza is held for the first time, in recognition of African harvest festivals.

Investigate
Mental Math: How old is Kwanza?

DECEMBER 27
1571

Johannes Kepler is born in Wurttemberg, Germany. Called "the father of modern astronomy," Kepler was considered one of the world's greatest astronomers. Kepler figured out that the planets travel in ellipses, not circles, around the Sun. In 1619, Kepler published some interesting tiling designs.

Investigate
Construct some tiling designs using geometric figures. The shapes must fit together perfectly, without any overlapping or any gaps.

1932

Radio City Music Hall opens, in New York's Rockefeller Center; it has 6,200 seats. A huge Wurlitzer organ and a 100-piece orchestra accompany vaudeville acts. The theatre didn't attract big crowds until it began screening movies and introduced the dancers known as the Rockettes.

Investigate
How many student bodies the size of your school's can be seated in Radio City Music Hall at the same time?

I'm a combination of rubber with other articles.

December 28, 1869
Chewing gum is patent #98304.

DECEMBER 28
1869

Patent number 98,304 is issued to William Semple, of Mount Vernon, Ohio, for chewing gum. He describes it as the "combination of rubber with other articles."

Investigate
Mental Math: How old is chewing gum?

1942

Captain Robert Oliver Daniel Sullivan completes his hundredth trip across the Atlantic Ocean. This one is from New York to Lisbon, Portugal. The first one was January 23, 1938, from New York to Marseilles, France.

Investigate
Assuming his trips were fairly evenly spaced, about how many trips did Captain Sullivan make across the Atlantic every year? every month?

DECEMBER 29
1848

Gaslights are installed in the White House. You can visit the White House online at *http://www.whitehouse.gov.*

Investigate
The White House has 132 rooms. How many lighting fixtures do you think there are? Make a reasonable estimate and then research the actual number.

1967

Physics professor John Wheeler coins the term *black hole* to describe a star that has undergone complete gravitational collapse. This is the final stage in the life history of a star.

There are a number of sites giving the latest information about black holes, including *http://antwerp/gsfc.nasa.gov/apod/black holes.html* and *http://cfpa.berkeley.edu/BHfaq .html.*

Investigate
Mental Math: How many years ago was this term coined?

DECEMBER 30
1776

General George Washington orders his 1,600 men to cross the Delaware River for the third time in three days, in order to join 3,000 militiamen on the New Jersey side. It is so cold and the soldiers have so little clothing that three men freeze to death during the crossing. When the remaining men arrive at their new camp, Washington promises a $10 bonus to anyone who will agree to stay for six weeks after their enlistment expires. No one accepts. Then one soldier steps forward. He is followed by 1,200 others. By the summer of 1777, the Patriot army has grown to 16,000.

Investigate
Mental Math: How many men were under Washington's command after the crossing?

1972

At latitude 59 north, longitude 29 west, the British ship *Weather Reporter* measures a wave 86 feet high in the North Atlantic. On the night of February 6, 1933, a sea wave was calculated at 112 feet from trough to crest, measured during a 68-knot hurricane from the U.S.S. *Ramapo*, traveling from Manila, in the Philippines, to San Diego, California.

Investigate
Find three things in your school that measure 100 to 112 feet.

DECEMBER 31

1947

Four hundred police are called out to control the screaming crowds at a Frank Sinatra concert in New York City.

Investigate

Mental Math: How many years ago did these teens go mad for Frank?

1989

According to the U.S. Bureau of Census, the median birth weight of babies born in the United States this year is 7 pounds, 7 ounces.

Investigate

What was the median, mean, and mode birth weight of the students in your class?